MADE IN DENMARK

MADE IN DENMARK

A picture-book about modern Danish Arts and Crafts

By Arne Karlsen and Anker Tiedemann

Published 1960 by Jul. Gjellerup, Copenhagen

4

INTRODUCTION *By Esbjørn Hiort, Director of 'Den Permanente', Copenhagen*

It is generally believed that we are more interested today in the design of articles of daily use than earlier generations were. But this is quite wrong. People have always wanted their daily tools to be both suitable and handsome.

The reason we think we are more interested in these things today is that we *talk* and *write* much more about the problems of design. The very natural reason for this is that we have lost contact with things to a certain extent. In the so-called good old days when handicraft traditions formed the firm basis of design and when clothes and utility wares were made at home everyone knew about materials and how they should be employed. Therefore, people could easily judge whether a thing was good or bad, whether naturally formed and of good materials – and of course everyone could see whether it was 'in style' because style didn't change so quickly then as it does nowadays.

But things are different today. Since the advent of the industrial revolution almost all production has passed to factories, and between producer and consumer there are, in addition, several middle-men. We no longer go to the tailor, the shoemaker, the cabinet-maker, etc. and order things 'to measure', ourselves choosing the materials, the size and the style. We buy our things 'ready made' in whatever way the manufacturers make them and often we hardly know what they are made of – for who can judge artificial materials and imitations?

If we are not entirely to lose contact with things – and thereby the pleasure they give us – we are simply forced to interest ourselves in them. We must *know* something about them. We must learn to appreciate quality when we meet it and to refuse poor quality and shams. We must come to *like* things that are good. This is an essential requirement in a material culture such as ours.

This is exactly the aim of this book; it purposes to tell us how things are made, why they are good. The two authors would like us to like the things they like – and which they know something about. Therefore it is not only an amusing book but also a useful one.

5

Kay Bojesen understood the child's need of using his imagination; he liked children because they could conjure up a brindle cow from a simple speckled stone. His toy animals are therefore elementary forms which every child can understand: sometimes angular, sometimes well rounded, often simply wooden blocks which a single cut of the knife has given the characteristics of an animal. They are all pleasant to grasp. Through his fine wooden toys made of good materials he has smuggled the first slight realization of quality into many a child.

The playthings shown here are part of a set called the 'Danish farm' from 1939. The box of blocks on wheels, made of beechwood in natural color, was designed in 1935.

CHAPTER ONE: ABOUT OUR FEELING FOR THINGS

The day we started to plan this book we sat opposite each other at a table on which drawings, photographs and our notes were spread about in an inspiring jumble.

On the floor in front of us sat the youngest son of the house who is not quite a year and a half old. Around him on the floor lay his favorite playthings: a large ball, a lidless cigar box, a number of wooden blocks and a stone. He grabbed after the things with his small, chubby hands and crowed delightedly when the stone banged against the bottom of the box or the ball ran away from him with small, lolloping hops. The child experiences things through his hands, becomes aware of the differences in their surfaces – whether they are rough or smooth, soft or hard.

The second son of the house, who is four years old, reacts somewhat differently to the concrete world about him. For him it is essential that things resemble something – though this does not mean that his choicest possessions are miniature replicas of autos and horses and weapons of war. On the contrary, like his little brother he prefers things of dimension and weight, things that demand an effort to handle them. But for him they are no longer simply form and mass, they have become symbols of things he has observed in the larger world outside his playroom. Through his imagination the things have acquired entity. The blocks, stones and bits of wood have become houses, human beings and animals. Through them he relives what he has already experienced and experiences new things with their help.

The oldest brother is seven. For him it is no longer enough that his favorites among inanimate things are passive. In his relation to them it is of the first importance that he and they together can accomplish something; they must be able to increase the possibilities of his hands to make 'things'. A light-weight hammer, a small saw and a screwdriver have become part of his daily life and the fact that he is beginning to understand how things are made adds to the pleasure they give him. He is the *functionalist* among the children; his respect for things is gauged by their practical qualities.

And we grown-ups, how do we react to things? Most of us have spent a number of years in building up a home. We have surrounded ourselves with hundreds of objects and have become attached to them just as children become attached to their playthings. Imperceptibly these things have become part of our existence. When we clear everything out of a room to make ready for the painter or paper-hanger, it is difficult to conceive the empty room as part of our home. Without things in them houses are, at best, architecture; they can never be *homes*.

We have acquired some of our belongings without any personal effort – things we have inherited or things we prize because they were given to us by someone we are fond of – but most of our possessions we have *chosen* ourselves. And that fact, alone, gives us a personal relation to them. We vouch for them and they tell something about us. We chose them not only because we realized that they would be useful in our daily lives but also because we felt they were connected with us in some mysterious way that is hard to define.

We must admit that our evaluation of things is based on much more complicated considerations than those which make a little boy fond of his ball. It is quite true that the child's experiences survive in the man and it sometimes happens that, at a mature age, we still make our choice with the spontaneity of the child. But usually our judgment is dependent on the innumerable external influences to which we have been exposed. Parents, school, professional training, spouse, everything and everybody we have met and much of what we have read have left their stamp on us and made the whole much less easy to comprehend.

We live in an age in which it is difficult for man to find firm foundations on which to base his convictions. This is true not only of the vital questions which affect our relations to others in religion and politics but also of smaller matters, such as our relation to inanimate things.

We can hardly reproach anyone for this. We can only regret that the men who pioneered the industrial revolution were so engrossed in technical development that they entirely forgot to safeguard the intangible values which lie hidden in the borderland between the purely material and the wholly artistic. Industry in the nineteenth century and at the beginning of the twentieth reduced the quality of the applied arts to a level of broad mediocrity and as a result people lost a sense of quality which, earlier, seems to have been taken for granted.

The situation on the whole has changed very little since then. Even among the highest intellects in our civilization today we find this strange lack of feeling for the quality of things. The ordinary man in technically underdeveloped countries often surrounds himself with objects which, as regards artistic quality and workmanship, are far superior to similar articles in the homes of cultivated persons in our part of the world. In-dustrialization and specialization have blunted our senses in many ways.

It is therefore with good reason that idealistic architects, designers, art historians, critics and others have sought to reconquer some of the lost territory by means of exhibitions, associations, magazine articles and books, and to obtain a foothold for mankind in a new and better founded conception of form and design. But unhappily this well meant activity has often had an unfortunate secondary effect: all the theorizing about form and beauty has too often made us feel – quite groundlessly – some-what ashamed to own things that deviate from the conventional taste but which we nevertheless highly prize. By emphasizing the artistic element to the exclusion of all else, the propaganda has created a certain mistrust between the things and us because artistic standards are so difficult to determine.

The present book is an attempt to establish confidence between the reader and the things that surround him. Our starting point will be a selection of modern Danish design; we will tell about the real and practical qualities of these things but will not delve into historical backgrounds or æsthetic theories.

The reader who expects sensational pronouncements of æsthetic character will be disappointed. The only expression of the authors' personal relations to the æsthetics of Danish design lies latent in the selection we have been forced to make. We have no desire to preach but will confine ourselves entirely to showing the things as they are.

In this attitude there is a challenge to the reader: *we* hope to arouse *you* to form your own judgment in each individual case.

CHAPTER TWO: ABOUT HANDICRAFT AND INDUSTRY

Applied art is customarily divided up in handicrafts and industrial art. As things have developed, however, it has become more and more difficult to place producers definitely in one category or the other. Today there are few handicraft workshops which make such exclusive wares that they can afford to ignore the economic advantages of an efficiently organized mass production. Most of them employ machinery to a larger or smaller extent.

The distinction must rather be sought in the human element, in the differences in qualifications and aims which separate the artist-craftsman from the industrial designer. The artist-craftsman is primarily a craftsman, just as the smith, the mason and the carpenter are. Like them he has served his apprenticeship in his trade. But while all other craftsmen work mainly from the drawings or specifications of others, the artist-craftsman designs his things himself. Often he also produces and sells them.

As a result of this he occupies an exceptional position among craftsmen in general and it gives his relation to the public a special character. Through direct contact with the consumer and through his creative ability his name is known. He has emerged from the anonymity of handicraft.

The industrial designer has seldom been trained in a particular trade or to work with a specific material. He is very often an architect or engineer who, through special studies, has become qualified to supervise and coordinate the complicated processes on which industrial production is based. Thus, while the artist-craftsman, with his own hands, follows his product from raw material to finished form, the designer is the leader of a working *team*.

The working methods of the artist-craftsman are, on the whole, the same today as they have been for centuries. The potter's wheel and the weaver's loom have the same construction as those our forefathers used, the silversmith's workbench and tools have not changed form. Neither has the basket-weaver's equipment.

In the picture are pieces of earthernware made by Grethe Lindblad photographed in her workshop.

Thus, while the artist-craftsman's work is based on ancient tradition, the industrial designer stands in the midst of an explosive development in which new manufacturing techniques and new materials are constantly turning up.

The economic backgrounds are likewise essentially different for the artist-craftsman and the industrial designer. While the craftsman's tools are few and simple, the working methods of large-scale production demand complicated tools and expensive machinery. And while the craftsman can always improve a not entirely satisfactory first result in the following examples, an industrial production cannot be altered without great difficulty and economic loss. Therefore the designer's preparatory work must be extremely thorough and take everything into consideration: production techniques, plant costs, storage, packaging, transportation, and many other problems which go far beyond the functional and æsthetic qualities of the product in question. Furthermore, the finished product must be able to satisfy demand for a long time in order that the investment in experiments and special equipment can be made to pay. Passing vagaries of fashion must therefore be avoided. Thus, the self-disciplin which the good artist-craftsman naturally exercises in regard to momentary style trends has become an absolute necessity in mass production, a tenet of its functional program.

The independent artist-craftsman is a private tradesman who organizes his production as he thinks best; he himself weighs the chances of the bearing capacity of his artistic intentions in relation to saleability. If his judgment is wrong the economic risk is his own.

The designer, on the other hand, stands between the consumer and the manufacturer. And at the same time the manufacturer is his employer, the one who pays for his work. But even though it is, naturally, the industrial firm alone that determines the designer's working conditions, it is, before all else, the designer's moral duty to protect the interests of the consumer in the manufacture of the product. In his work he must not only keep in step with technical development but also with development in the living standard of the population so that the demands which have created his work may be satisfactorily met.

The industrial designer does not only work with the external appearance of things but often also with technical problems which, on the face of it, one would expect the technical staff to solve: rationalization of production, simplification of stockroom work, reduction of storage space, etc. The pictures above show how the designer's work with the manufacturing process and storing problems has reduced the number of fittings of a coffee pot from eighteen to six. In the new model he has also made it possible to raise and lower the lid with the thumb of the hand holding the pot. Furthermore, the handle is designed so that it can also be used on other things (e.g. the water and milk jugs on page 115).

Both pots are of aluminum with handles and knobs of black bakelite; the new model was designed by Erik Herløw for Dansk Aluminium, Inc.

13

That by doing this he is also serving the best interests of the manufacturer it has until recently been difficult to make the latter understand. The manufacturers felt that the primary job of the designer was to give their products novel form – to 'stylize' them – in order to increase sales as rapidly and effectively as possible. It was not his business, they insisted, to make the products more efficient.

Fortunately, this attitude has now almost entirely disappeared. In recent years the designer has taken his natural place in many of our industries, including some which are outside the field of industrial art. He has become the deliberate coordinator of the collaboration among many different persons which is necessary to obtain a perfect industrial product. Today he not only acts as the intermediary between consumer and manufacturer but also coordinates the contributions of technicians, artisans and salesmen in the planning of production. He is no longer called in at the last stage to give the final polish or decoration to a product after the materials have been selected and the technical problems solved. He now takes part in the industrial process from the very beginning and must therefore not only possess the analytical and creative abilities of the artist-craftsman but also the will to cooperate, organizational talent and tirelessness.

In the following pages the reader will be given the opportunity to see the individual artist-craftsman at work – the craftsman who makes the things with his own hands in a workshop he shares with fellow craftsmen and the master craftsman whose business, though based on handwork, is conducted more or less on factory principles, producing small quantities of the same articles and with a designer attached to the workshop. Finally we shall visit a number of large industries. Individually, each visit will give a short description of the trade in question and together the thirteen workshops we enter will give us a detailed picture of the production apparatus at the disposal of Danish craftsmen and designers, apparatus which they have learned to utilize to the utmost both artistically and technically.

In the potter's kiln the simple clay is transformed into pots. On the opposite page are seen a number of earthernware articles made by Gutte Eriksen and photographed in her electric kiln.

THE POTTER

In Nathalie Krebs' person the experimental chemist is united with the ceramic artist. She combines the chemist's knowledge of the material with the potter's feeling for it. In her workshop 'Saxbo' she has always sought to produce wares of uniformly high quality. Without lowering her standards in any way she has succeeded in giving that breadth to her production which is necessary in order to produce the individual piece of work at a reasonable price.

Despite its size, Saxbo has been able to preserve the close contact between artist and product which is otherwise the forte of the small workshop. Behind each piece of pottery from Saxbo's kilns stands its creator, and even though it owes its glaze to Nathalie Krebs, each individual piece is marked by the intention and artistic will of the artist-craftsman who made it.

Many of Denmark's leading potters have been associated with Saxbo but the special character of its production is due primarily to Eva Stæhr-Nielsen and Edith Sonne Bruun. Today, the youngest member of the staff is the potter Kirsten Weeke. On the opposite page we see her at the potter's wheel at work on the teapot which we shall watch grow out of the wet clay. To the right is Nathalie Krebs preparing the glaze.

The potter's most important material is clay, an unimpressive substance in its natural state completely lacking textural beauty. Nevertheless it has certain attributes which have made it a patient servitor of mankind. When softened with water it can be thrown, modelled or cast in almost every shape imaginable. And after drying it retains that shape while firing increases its strength and hardness.

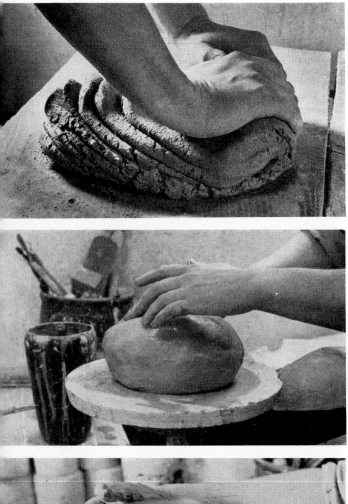

Clay can be used in its natural state; for earthenware the blue clay rich in chalk or the ferruginous red clay is used. Kirsten Weeke employs a so-called stoneware mixture which contains fire-clay, kaolin, feldspar and quartz to which she has added crushed, baked fire-clay, partly to prevent shrinkage of the pot during drying, partly to emphasize its robust form through the coarse, slightly rough surface it produces.

Before throwing the clay is kneaded as shown in the top picture. With a large, gliding motion in which the entire weight of the body from the waist up is put behind the pressure of the palms on the lump of clay, the potter forces the clay out in cakes which are again gathered together and again pressed out. After doing this several times she has a lump of clay ready for the wheel, that is, plastic and homogeneous, free from air-holes and other irregularities. In the middle picture the lump of clay is thrown with great force down on the disk, as near the center as possible. In the bottom picture Kirsten Weeke has kicked the wheel into motion.

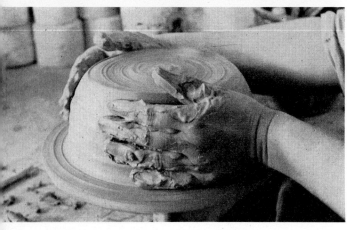

The lump of clay rotates slowly between her wet hands until it adheres firmly to the center and no longer spreads out. Only when this is done can the actual throwing begin.

During the entire process the wheel is kept in motion at a fair rate of speed by means of rhythmic, precise kicks against the footplate. (See picture page 16).

18

The thumb of the right hand slowly disappears into the revolving mass. With strong, uniform pressure the thumb bears down making an indentation in the clay which is quickly widened. The fingers of the left hand keep the hole open.

The position of the hands changes. With the left hand pressed against the inner wall of clay and the right against the outer wall, the clay is gradually drawn up. The motion is repeated from the bottom towards the top. The walls are thinned out by pressing evenly with the two index fingers. The clay begins to come alive.

The clay has now been brought up to the desired height and the walls are of the required thickness. The entire process looks simple and easy; the cylinder seems to have risen quite effortlessly from the lump of clay but actually this throwing process requires a great deal of experience.

A teapot grows out of the cylinder. While the cylinder revolves Kirsten Weeke presses the wall into the shape she desires. Both hands are in constant motion round the body of the pot. With her right thumb she forms the 'shoulder'.

The speed is reduced during the last rotations, the shape is adjusted in accordance with a model based on Kirsten Weeke's original design. The body of the pot is finished and is severed from the disk with the help of a piece of wire.

The pot is well turned. In its form we are immediately aware of the forces which the potter has employed: the centrifugal force which forced the material out from the center and the gravitational pull which limited the outward curve of the sides. Signs of the rotation appear on the surface of the body in the slight traces left by the potter's fingers.

The lid and spout are thrown and the two 'ears' to which the handle will be attached together with a support on the back of the pot are formed. After the half-dried body has been treated with a smoothing iron, the contact surface of the material is roughened and the parts attached to the body with a paste-like clay called 'slip'.

20

The pot is now ready to be fired and glazed. After drying it is placed in an electric kiln in a temperature of 1650° F until it becomes red-hot. This hardens the clay but it still remains porous enough to absorb the glaze. The glazing is done by immersing the pot in a glaze solution.

Now the exciting period approaches. The glazed wares are carefully stacked in the kiln; they must not touch each other or come in direct contact with the flame and are therefore protected by capsules of fire-proof clay. The kiln is then lit.

During one and a half days Nathalie Krebs' and the firing-master's entire attention is concentrated on the kiln. They seldom leave Saxbo's large, cylindrical-shaped firing hall. The kiln is stoked with coal; the flames lick the protecting capsules. In the firing vitrification takes place.

After 36 hours – when the temperature has risen to 2400° F – firing is stopped and the kiln allowed to cool for two days. Now the moment has come when the kiln door can be opened. The results of weeks of work are removed one by one from the black depths of the kiln.

The potter's work is unpredictable. The flame bath can transform the humble clay and the insipid glaze solution to a marvel of textural beauty but it can also melt the entire contents of the kiln into a worthless lump of lava. Here, the firing has been a success, the excitement followed by relief. The glaze sparkles in grayish green and brown, sober but vital. Material, form and glaze are in perfect balance.

24

THE WEAVER

Vibeke Klint's weaving workshop is in an old stable behind one of the great houses on the shore road between Copenhagen and Elsinore. From her east window she has a view of Sweden on the opposite shore of the Sound.

Vibeke Klint is unique in her strong and sober devotion to her art. Her work has special weight because she is one of the very few who are able to stick to the best of tradition and at the same time add something which is young and entirely her own. And this is true both of technical and artistic tradition.

Vibeke Klint was trained by Gerda Henning, one of the pioneers of modern Danish weaving.

After Gerda Henning's death in 1951 Vibeke Klint took over her workshop and since then has woven fabrics for private persons and public institutions. She also designs fabrics for the Danish textile industry.

On the following pages we shall watch her work on a silk dress fabric.

The weaver's material is not, like the potter's, a raw material that can be used in its natural state. The yarn, whether silk or wool, cotton or linen, has gone through a long series of processes before it lies, ready to be used, on the weaver's yarn shelves. It has been cleaned, carded, spun, twisted, and often also dyed.

25

Vibeke Klint does not weave from drawings; a colored drawing can be an excellent basis for the working out of, for example, a rug pattern with homogeneous color planes but for a narrow-striped fabric like the dress material here a drawing does not give a sufficiently good impression of what the finished fabric will look like. Samples made by winding the yarns on small pieces of cardboard are much better. In this way the weaver can work out her color scheme and the number of threads of each color that are necessary to obtain the effect she desires.

In the picture at the top of the page are seen a number of such samples.

The threads which serve as the longitudinal skeleton of the fabric are called the warp, the transverse threads the weft. The warp is fed to the loom from a 'warping-mill' consisting of two rectangular wooden frames at right angles to each other so they can turn on a vertical axis.

In the picture above the top of the warping-mill is seen at the left.

As a rule it is expedient to feed out several threads of the warp at a time. They are passed through a flat, perforated board and fastened to two 'lease rods' at the top of the warping-mill which is then set in motion, anti-clockwise, so that the threads, guided by the perforated board, are led into an angular spiral down over the two wooden frames. When the desired warp-length is reached the threads are wound round a wooden peg on the lower frame and the warping-mill set in motion in the opposite direction so that the threads run along the spiral back to the lease rods. This operation is continued until the right number of warp threads are wound round the frames. When the warp threads are taken off the mill they are crocheted into a thick braid. In the picture at the right Vibeke Klint is preparing the weft. The yarn is wound round a short, thin tube of paper.

The setting of the loom calls for great dexterity and unremitting attention. The warp threads are wound, evenly disposed in the required width, around a solid wooden warp-beam at the back of the loom. The warp threads from the two lease rods on the warping-mill are divided into two lots and the threads of each lot are passed through 'eye-holes' in a system of controls called heddles (small pieces of yarn with openings for the warp threads to pass through). The heddles are hung on shafts which are again hung up to form a leverage system, operated by foot, by which the weaver can alternately raise and lower the two lots of heddles to achieve the 'under and over' which is the basis of weaving.

In the picture to the left the warp-beam is seen at the bottom of the photograph; to the left can be seen the warp threads that have already been put through the heddles, to the right the yarn still to be put through. The horizontal wooden bars on this side of the heddles lie in the shed (the opening made between the threads of the warp by the motion of the heddles for the shuttle to pass through). From the heddles the warp threads pass through a 'reed' which is placed in the 'batten' (a movable bar which closes the weft) and the threads are then tied to the cloth-roller in front of the loom. It is this roller on which the finished fabric will be rolled.

In the top picture on the opposite page Vibeke Klint is pushing the batten with the reed in it to its backmost position so that the shed through which the shuttle is cast can be seen. In the bottom picture the shuttle is lying on the part of the fabric already finished.

The shuttle is shaped like a torpedo; its surface is even and smooth and its point lifts so that it easily glides over the layer of warp threads. It surrounds the bobbin on two sides so that the weft thread cannot get stuck in the warp threads. When shuttling, the weft thread runs off the bobbin and settles in place in the shed.

28

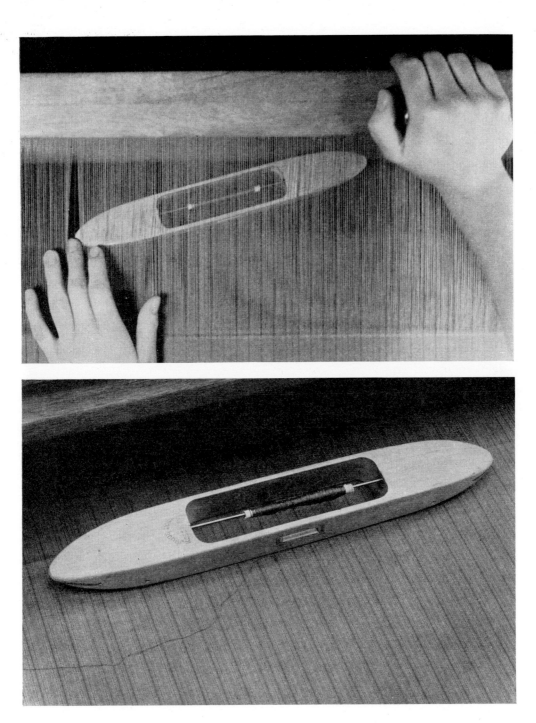

The great amount of preparatory work and the laborious setting of the loom – which is quite simple in principle – ends with an uncomplicated working process: the weaving itself, which is illustrated in the two final pictures of this series. In the picture above the batten – as in the picture on the preceding page – is in its backmost position. With the help of the heddle shafts at the left the warp threads are separated in two layers so that a triangular opening – the shed – appears between them. The shuttle is cast in from the right selvedge, the right hand grasps the batten

and the left hand catches the shuttle when it reaches the left selvedge.

In the picture on the opposite page the newly laid 'pick' – the weft thread cast by the shuttle – is being packed firmly against that which preceded it with the help of the batten. The batten is then swung back, the heddles shifted by foot and the shuttle cast in from the left. This process continues until the fabric is finished.

The experienced weaver is one with her loom, every one of her movements occur in a smooth working rhythm. Her feet raise and lower the

warp threads, her hands swing the batten back and forth and direct the swift flight of the shuttle through the shed. The pick settles in place next to the foregoing one and the fabric grows in length in front of the reed. The forceful stroke of the batten against the pick falls in a measured rhythm.

The weaving technique described here is the simplest possible. The weft thread goes over one warp thread, under the next, over the next, under the next, and so on until the selvedge is reached. On they way back it goes over where before it

went under and under where it went over. This is called plain weaving. But the loom of course holds innumerable combination possibilities. The warp and weft can be woven together in the most intricate ways, the pick can be closely packed or loosely disposed, yarns of varying thickness and structure can be combined, the weft can cover the warp, or the warp cover the weft.

There is hardly a limit to the possible variations. Rugs, upholstery, garment fabrics, curtains can all be produced on the same simple loom.

31

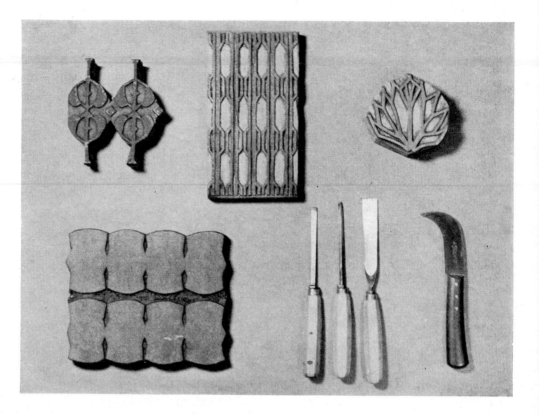

THE TEXTILE PRINTER

The young textile printer Dorte Raaschou has in her own quiet way made a name for herself in modern Danish textile design.

In her little workshop high up under the roof in an old apartment house in Copenhagen she has created, with simple tools, a series of very exclusive fabrics, especially suitable for dresses and curtains. Her patterns are usually composed of a repetition of one or two small motives which, when disposed in various ways in relation to each other and partially over each other, cover the surface in a simple and discreet design.

She takes her motives from Nature, finding them by studying plants, animals and stones, but before they reach the printing table she has worked so much with them that they have become ornaments with no clear reminiscences of their origin.

Dorte Raaschou's colors are subdued and delicate; used in the composition's rhythmic repetition of a trim little motive, they endow her artistic expression with femininity and charm. In many fabrics Dorte Raaschou combines block and screen printing, textile printing's two main techniques. The dress material we shall here watch her produce is characterized by this combination.

The line drawing in the pattern is carried out in screen printing. For her stencil she uses fine silk gauze stretched over a wooden frame. The design is drawn on the silk with chalk which produces a very oily stroke. Thereafter a liquid gum is poured over the silk so that the undesigned parts are 'stopped out'. As the chalk repels water, the fluid does not cling to the chalk design. When the liquid gum has dried the chalk is removed with terpentine so that the design is seen as openings in the membrane of gum. Finally the stencil is strengthened by brushing it over with varnish. To prevent the varnish from covering the lines of the design it is absorbed with the help of a piece of cloth from the underside of the silk.

For the printing Indigosol dyes are used. They are applied to the stencil with the help of a 'doctor', a rubber strip fitted into a broad handle.

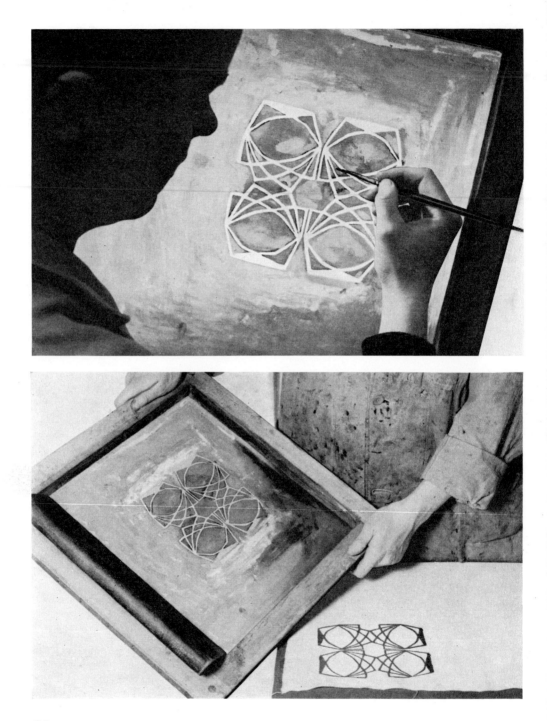

In the top picture on the preceding page Dorte Raaschou is giving the final touches to the finished screen. The design appears as white lines in the layer of varnish in places where the dye can be absorbed. In the bottom picture Dorte Raaschou has printed the first motive; the doctor is still lying on the frame.

The second and third motives in the pattern are block printed. In this technique the design is carved in wood or linoleum. (The picture on page 32 shows several of Dorte Raaschou's printing blocks together with the tools she uses in carving.) As a rule in block printing the dye is applied by means of a pad or roller but Dorte Raaschou uses a brush which makes it possible to vary the interplay of the colors by coating some parts with a thick layer of the dye, others with a thin layer.

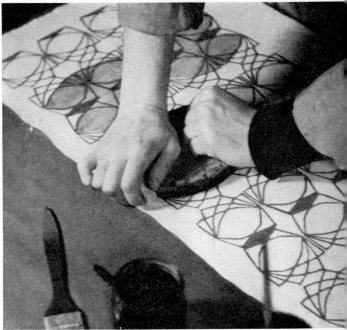

In the little picture above Dorte Raaschou is brushing the dye on the block; at top right she places it with meticulous care — though by eye measurement alone — on the fabric and in the bottom picture she is pressing the block firmly against the fabric with her entire weight.

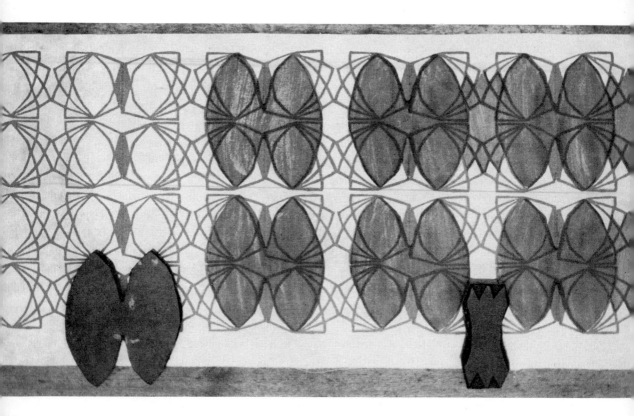

Above, we see the three stages of the printing: first the line drawing is printed by screen printing and then the pattern is elaborated by the addition of two block-printed motives.

After drying, the colors are fixed in a weak solution of sulphuric acid; the acid is then neutralized in a soda bath and finally the fabric is boiled in soap water.

When the dyes are fixed they change color. For example, a green dye becomes red when fixed. Therefore the textile printer must train herself, by innumerable experiments, to work with her pattern in an entirely different color scheme than the one she is aiming at.

On the opposite page the complete pattern is seen printed on silk in violet, apricot and dusty green colors.

Even in the picture we feel that the colors do not lie on the surface of the cloth, as on a painter's canvas, but are absorbed in the fibers of the material. The application of the dyes has not stiffened the silk; it can still fall in graceful folds in a dress or curtain. As in all good yard-goods' printing, the pattern is such that the material can be cut off or draped without mutilating the design.

On the contrary, soft folds will only enrich the effect of the printed pattern.

36

THE SILVERSMITHY

Henning Koppel is a sculptor. His work most distinctively expresses an aspect of Danish silver which, during the past few decades, has laid more and more stress on the purely æsthetic side of design. In most of his work functional fulfillment is secondary, dominated by an original and personal form which is ostensibly based on function but in which the sculptural expression has become an end in itself.

The jug which we are going to watch the silversmith make on the following pages costs over a thousand dollars retail. "Therefore", Koppel himself has said, "no one buys it exclusively to use for water or milk; silver work of this kind

must have an independent artistic value that raises it above ordinary utility wares."

The jug is made in Georg Jensen's silversmith workshop which is the largest in Denmark. But despite all production efficiency it is made exclusively by hand. It is produced by one man alone from the moment the shears make the first cut in the sheet of silver to the moment when the completed jug is given its final finish.

Silver is an expensive material but, employed in the right way, it is also unsurpassed. To date, for instance, no set of stainless steel cutlery can bear comparison with silver cutlery. And also for larger objects silver as a material has no equal. It is durable, it is malleable, it can be shaped into almost every imaginable form and its surface, when correctly treated, has great textural beauty.

Raw silver is imported into Denmark in bars, sheets, wire or 'beads' (small drops of chemically pure silver that are produced in the same way children make tiny balls of wax by dropping melted wax in cold water. The bag in the picture is full of such beads). In Georg Jensen's workshop sterling silver alone is used which contains a very small percentage of copper and only one-tenth of one per cent of impurities (including ash from the refining process).

39

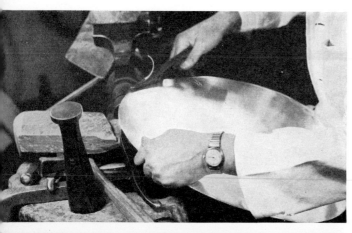

1st day: The jug is made from sheet silver 1 mm thick which is cut with plate shears. The silversmith works at a solid workbench with a semicircular front before each working place. Under this a piece of leather is suspended which catches the small bits of silver that fall from the article being shaped. Each smith has at his disposal a vise and a large wooden block heavy enough to hold anvils of various sizes and shapes.

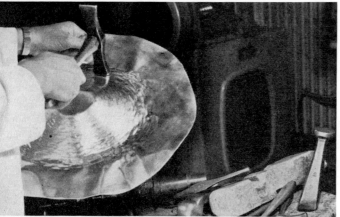

On the basis of Koppel's original sketch — reproduced opposite the title page in this book — and a plaster model an exact drawing is made and with this in front of him the silversmith begins to hammer the disk of silver into shape. During the preliminary hammering he uses a block of wood for a foundation. In this picture the bottom of the jug is growing out of the silver disk.

3rd day: As the curves gradually become larger the silversmith hammers the edge of the disk in pleats and then hammers them together again to a more closed form in which the material is thicker. After hammering for some time tension arises in the material which must be relieved or the silver will split. This is done by heating it red-hot with a blow torch.

40

10th day: After tens of thousands of light hammer taps the main lines of the jug slowly begin to appear. As yet it resembles an open, symmetrical vase. The silversmith now exchanges the wooden block for a little anvil of a special type.

14th day: The shape is beginning to close. The steel anvil has now been replaced by a long iron introduced through the neck opening. During the shaping the silversmith uses a large number of hammers, each one with a different shaped head according to its purpose, and all of different weights.

20th day: After many hours of patient hammering the body of the jug is roughly shaped. It has been given its characteristic contours and all curves and lines have been carefully inspected to see that they precisely follow the working drawing. To remove the traces of the many hammer taps on the body of the jug the silversmith first uses a broad-faced 'planishing' or smoothing hammer and then a file. The silver that is filed off is carefully collected.

24th day: The handle is sawed from a sheet of silver and closed lengthwise over a wooden form. It is soldered together to an angular tube with a diminishing cross-section toward the ends. It is then filled with pitch so the tube can be worked up without collapsing. When the handle has been given its final shape the pitch is melted out.

25th day: The finished handle is wired to the jug and then soldered in place. Finally the jug is given its final finish with silver polish on a felt pad (picture at bottom of page).

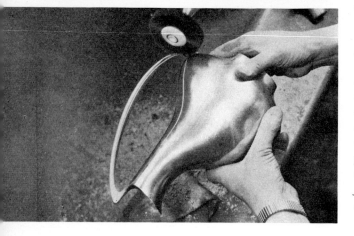

Opposite is the finished jug; it is 25 cm high and weighs over two pounds. The silversmith has worked on it almost one month and thereby everything has been done to make it as perfect a piece of craftsmanship as possible. With its supple curves, its aristocratic appearance and lovely subdued sheen it is not only a jug but a piece of sculpture, not only a useful object but a work of art. As a commodity, according to Danish standards, it is only for the wealthy few. But as an artistic and textural experiment, work of this character has significance far beyond the individual article. The experience Koppel has gained in his silver sculpture has been of great importance for his later work of more utilitarian character. Thus, he has designed a distinctly functional set of flat silver which owes its æsthetic appeal to his experience as a sculptor in that material.

43

THE WORKER IN SILVER

Kay Bojesen, who died in 1958, became world famous as the maker of wooden toys (see page 6) but nevertheless he was first and foremost a silversmith. His original training was in the silversmith craft and it was there – despite all success in other fields – he made his greatest contribution.

Therefore his silver is still being produced. In old houses in the neighborhood where he had his little basement shop silversmiths and silver workers are still producing Kay Bojesen's models just as when they worked for Bojesen himself. From among his many works we have chosen a silver casserolle to show here because both handwork and machine work enter into its manufacture.

The pictures on these pages show the work done by the silver-worker Aage Hinsch during the throwing up of the body. The material used is exactly the same as in Koppel's jug (page 40): 1 mm thick silver sheeting which here too is first cut in a disk. The throwing up is done on a lathe on which the disk is fastened against a wooden former of the same shape as the finished casserolle. As seen in the pictures the silver is held in place with the help of a wooden disk.

The lathe is set in motion and the silver-worker carefully forces the silver over the former. He

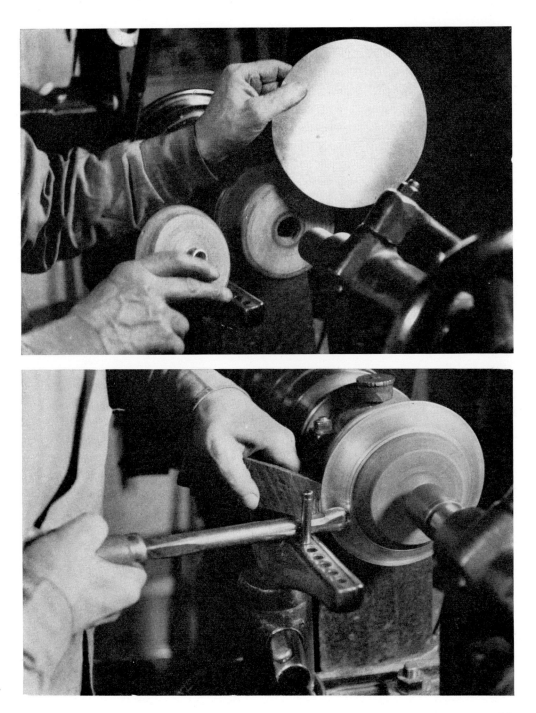

uses all his strength, hunching his back against the strap which binds him to the lathe. Slowly the silver wraps itself around the rotating former. With a steel instrument he forces the silver further on, at the same time controlling it with a wooden peg to prevent it from pleating or ruffling along the edge. At intervals he interrupts the work to relieve tension in the silver with the help of a gas flame.

Less than fifteen minutes after the lathe was started the silver has reached the opposite end of the former and the body is finished. In contrast to the hammered jug, the material here is of equal thickness throughout. The picture at the top of page 47 shows various wooden formers; the one used here is in the middle.

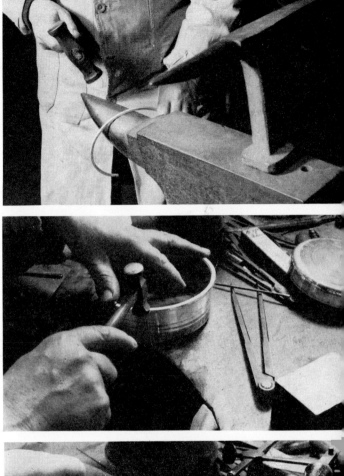

The finishing of the casserolle is done in the little basement workshop of the silversmith C. H. Jensen. Along the top edge he solders on a rim made of silver wire that is square in cross-section and then hammers it into shape over the pointed end of an anvil (top, right). He also makes a silver socket into which the rosewood handle will later be fitted (bottom, right).

In the picture on the opposite page at top the silversmith is cutting the wire for the rim in the required length with a little metal saw. Below is seen a close-up view of the workbench with its characteristic semi-circular front. Note the large piece of leather which forms a closed sack in which scraps of silver are collected. Also note the different shapes of the hammer-heads on the hammers in the foreground.

Though Kay Bojesen was very much an individualist he nevertheless formulated, through his work, the most lucid and personal expression of the conception that pure functional form should be the only aim of modern silver design. If silver is employed to make useful things that really are used, the daily wear and tear will make them even more beautiful, he insisted. And in one place he wrote: By using her silverware every day the housewife will discover to her delight that the once so hated task of silver polishing is no worse than any other housework. The surface of the metal should have innumerable scratches – thousands of tiny marks which only daily use and daily wear can give – thereby speedily bringing forth the whiteish, subdued sheen which is so characteristic of old silver.

Thus, silverware designed primarily for use was close to Bojesen's heart. His favorite articles were ordinary things like coffee and tea pots, sugar bowls and cream jugs and round casserolles like the one shown here, with such deep lids that they can be used independently as serving dishes. In his design beauty and function were united in clearly defined shapes but his things are never impersonal or austere, they are friendly and smiling, without sharp corners or angular profiles. His things are built up of few elements which individually have æsthetic functions beyond their purely practical ones. In this casserolle the soldered-on rim and the soft rim-profile hold the form together and make possible the play of light and shadow on the body.

In it the very nature of silver is revealed to us.

THE GLASS-WORKS

There is probably no material used in handicrafts more amazing than glass. Nor is any manufacturing process more fantastic than that which takes place in a glass-works or any handicraft more demanding than the glass-blower's. In Holmegaard's glass-works in the southern part of the island of Zealand generations of glass-blowers have followed one another in the same families. Surrounding the glass-works during the hundred and fifty years it has existed a small, closely-knit community has grown up whose entire existence is bound up with glass. Most of the craftsmen have been connected with the works since childhood; they have gone to Holmegaard's own grammar-school, as apprentices they have lent a hand when the glass-blowers were working with their blowing-irons and finally they themselves have taken up the hollow rod as fully trained journeymen.

Per Lütken, who is seen at his drawing-board at left, is the art director of the glass-works. Originally he was a painter but since 1942, when he joined Holmegaard, he has devoted himself to glass, a willing but at times also stubborn material. He has experimented with it, steadily coaxing new possibilities from the manufacturing process and using new techniques as the basis of his artistic contribution. In the following we will keep to the traditional process as it is used to produce a simple decanter but also here we will see that Per Lütken was inspired by the very special nature of the material.

The glass Holmegaard uses is made from fine sand rich in iron, which is imported from Holland, and of soda and a small quantity of red lead which gives the glass weight and its ringing sound and increases its transparency. The raw materials are blended to a soluble substance which is heated overnight in the great furnaces of the works until as a molten mass it has reached a temperature of 1450° C.

50

The scene in the 'glass-house', as it is called, is very picturesque. The glass-house is a large, unceilinged room which soars high up to the dimly seen rafters under the tiled roof. From the openings in the huge furnaces a fiery glow fills the room. Numerous boys pass and repass each other on the way from the stations at the furnaces to the large cooling ovens, carrying the finished but still glowing wares on long poles.

The glass-blower's work is pure handicraft but the making of a glass article is not carried out by one man alone; the working process is based on teams, each member of which has his special job to perform. A young journeyman (sitting in the background in the picture to the right) extracts a blob of the red-hot glass from the furnace on the end of a blowing-iron by turning the long, thin pipe round and round in the glowing mass until the blob is large enough. An apprentice then passes the blowing-iron to a glass-blower who shapes the blob in a shaping block – a large, deep-bowled wooden spoon. He rolls the viscous glass back and forth in the shaper, supporting the blowing-iron on his work-bench, until the blob is spherical in cross-section and the material evenly disposed in the shape of a slim pear.

Before the blob of glass is laid in the shaping block it is immersed in a tub of water so that a layer of steam arises between the glowing mass and the bowl of the spoon. This prevents any traces of the rotation being left on the surface of the glass.

When the blob is shaped the glass-blower rises from his bench and with the blowing-iron unceasingly rotating between his fingers he blows an air bubble into the soft mass; using eye-measurement only he blows the material into a sphere the size of the finished decanter. The final blowing is done with the help of a wooden mold which is first dipped in water. Due to the length of the blowing-iron (which is determined by the shortest distance from the blazing hot furnace at

53

which the blower can stand) the craftsman must stand on a little footstool when blowing into the mold while an apprentice opens and shuts the mold for him. During the blowing the iron is kept continuously rotating.

The decanter now sits on the end of the blowing-iron like a large, pear-shaped drop; with a precise blow over a steel rail the neck is severed from the blowing-iron and then an older apprentice fastens the decanter with a lump of molten glass to one end of a thin, solid, iron bar.

The neck of the decanter is now guided into an open reverberatory furnace until it again becomes soft and can be clipped into the right shape. The marks left by the shears are removed by heating it again and then the 'lip' is drawn down with the help of a pair of tongs as the iron bar holding the decanter is rolled back and forth over the iron rails on the workbench (see picture at top left). Finally the decanter is severed from the iron bar and brought to the cooling oven where, in the course of one-and-a-half hours, it is cooled from 800° C to ordinary room temperature.

The decanter's stopper is cast in a mold and the final stage in the manufacturing process is the fitting of the stopper to the decanter. The stopper is placed in a rotating spindle and with the help of carborundum emulsion it is bored into the neck of the decanter so that the two fit tightly together (bottom, left). Thus, each decanter has its own, specially fitted stopper and the owner of two of the decanters cannot count on the stoppers being interchangeable.

Opposite is seen the finished decanter. Its shape is like a large drop of water; the soft, glowing, molten glass, though now rigid, cold and hard, is still latent in its graceful lines.

56

THE CABINET-MAKER

For more than thirty years Copenhagen's Cabinet-Makers' Guild has held, in connection with its annual exhibition, open competitions for proposals for new furniture-types, an initiative that has been of inestimable value in the development of Danish furniture design. Collaboration with the many furniture designers has not only raised the standard of workmanship and design of hand-made furniture but the experiments that have been carried out and the experience gained have also been of great significance for the production of fine factory-made furniture.

Among the artists who have made a name for themselves as designers for the cabinet-makers, the chair designer par excellence is Hans J. Wegner. He is himself a trained furniture craftsman and therefore has a special feeling for wood, for its structural possibilities, its finishing and surface treatment. He often makes his models himself, in full size, repeating the same type again and again until he is entirely satisfied with the result. A chair is never put into production before he has tested it in his own home.

Wegner's chairs are sturdy and masculine, their dimensions are large and their edges and surfaces well rounded so that they can stand the wear and tear of daily use.

In form they combine tradition with originality.

Hans J. Wegner's handmade furniture is produced by the cabinet-maker Johannes Hansen whose workshop, though equipped with motor driven tools, maintains the highest standard of craftsmanship. And this standard begins with the material. Johannes Hansen himself selects the wood that is used in his furniture at the lumber-yards in Copenhagen's free harbor. Among the hundreds of planks available only a very small percentage meets his high standards. For the top-rail on the armchair we shall follow through his workshop the wood is selected with special care. A pile of choice planks of Bangkok teakwood is shown on the preceding page.

After having designed and redesigned the chair and after having made several models of it – first in small dimensions and later in full size – Hans Wegner combines the results of his experiments in a working drawing like the one reproduced on the opposite page. Here, all the construction details are clearly described on a scale of 1:1 for plan, section and elevation.

The underframe of the chair is made of Danish oak with turned legs and a seat frame containing rebates that hold the seat. The gluing of the frame is shown at the left.

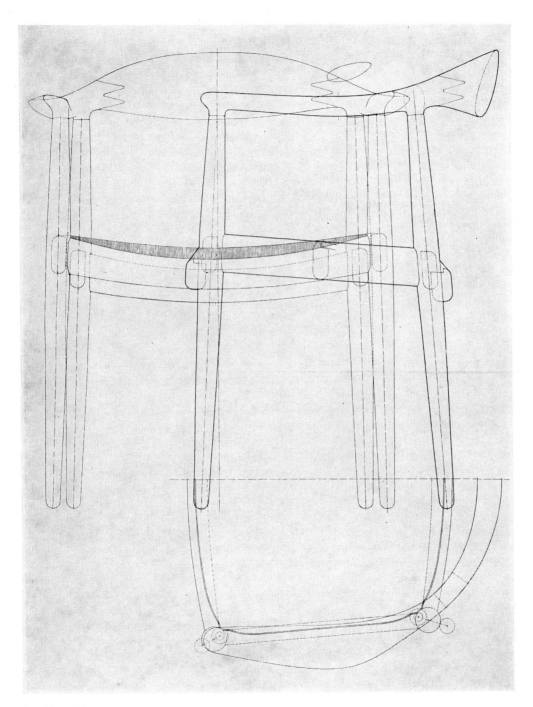

59

In this – as in so many of Hans J. Wegner's chair models – the shaping of the top-rail plays an important role; powerfully curved, vigorously modelled top-rails have become the characteristic element in his chairs. Their latent strength gives the chairs their artistic distinction.

The shaping of the top-rail calls for the greatest skill. It is done by eye-measurement with hand tools and the least uncertainty in the craftsman's feeling for the very tense curves would be catastrophic. Even the smallest divergence from the model would disturb the firmness of the contours.

The top-rail is fashioned from three pieces of teakwood. When the planks have been seasoned for between 6 months and a year they are cut up in rough-shaped pieces like the ones shown here. After cutting, the pieces are left in the drying-room for from 3 to 6 weeks and are then stored 10 months in order to become acclimatized.

By dividing the top-rail in three parts not only is better wood economy assured but the right veining is obtained. If the top-rail were carved out of one large plank the grain in some places would run across the rail which would essentially weaken it.

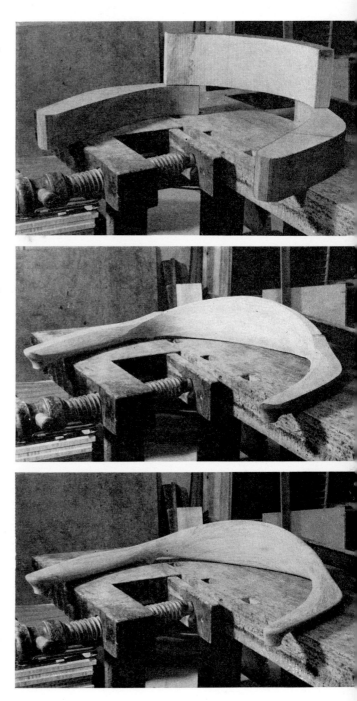

The three pieces are joined together in saw-tooth joints which are made on a cutting machine. By this method of joining the gluing surface of the joints is four times as large as in the end to end or butt joining, and therefore four times as strong. The preliminary rough shaping of the glued top-rail is done with a saw, chisel and file. One stage of this process is shown on the opposite page.

Finally the fine finishing of the top-rail is done with spoke shave, file and sandpaper.

61

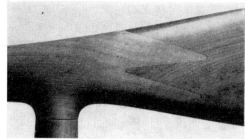

The spoke shave used in the finishing of the top-rail is an old French type which is no longer sold and therefore must be made by the craftsman himself (picture at left).

Above is shown the finished top-rail. It is not only structurally right but extremely decorative. Where the teakwood rail is joined to the oak frame each joint is marked, for æsthetic reasons, by a small, hollow chamfer.

On the opposite page the finished chair is seen with its upholstered seat covered with leather in natural color.

It was more than ten years ago that Hans J. Wegner designed this chair and Johannes Hansen exhibited it at the annual exhibition of the Copenhagen Cabinet-Maker's Guild but it is still being made in large numbers. In English-speaking countries it has become so popular that it is called simply 'the chair' — with the accent on 'the'. Few utility wares have attained such fame and therefore it is quite reasonable that with this chair we leave the field of handicrafts for characteristic examples of industrial art.

63

THE PORCELAIN FACTORY

The ceramic artist Axel Brüel is one of the few artist-craftsmen who, at a ripe age, allied himself with the ceramic industry and succeeded so well in adapting his art to machine production that today it lends itself naturally to industrial methods and industrial materials – in this case porcelain. In his own pottery Brüel has particularly occupied himself with form; glaze has always been of secondary importance to him. Therefore his glazes have no independent beauty; they are usually mat, dark and discreet, their only function being to give support to the volume of his wares. And even though Brüel has often employed extremely imaginative decoration, inspired by the art of primitive peoples, it has always been purely surface decoration, subordinate to and emphasizing the form.

This craftsmanlike cultivation of sculptural but very sober form has been of great advantage to Brüel in his later work with machine-produced articles of daily use. Without any great difficulty he has been able to disengage himself from the heavy forms of clay pottery and give to porcelain the stringency and precision of detail which is natural to that material.

In Brüel's coffee service 'Thermodan', which he designed for the porcelain factory Danmark, Inc., he has – in close collaboration with the factory's technical leader, Søren Berg, and the chief thrower, Roland Mortensen – created a set of *porcelain which not only marks a turning point in Brüel's personal production but also in the porcelain industry as a whole. It is a creative achievement both artistically and technically. The shape of the individual pieces is based on an analysis of the use and storing of a coffee service.*

Shaping a handle has always been a problem. Handles have a tendency to break off during firing, are often broken in transportation to shop or customer and are likewise easily damaged in washing. Furthermore, due to the handles, a coffee service takes up too much of the restricted space in kitchen cupboards.
But what about a service without handles? Could anything be devised to take their place?
By making the individual pieces so slim that it would be possible to get your hand around them, handles would no longer be necessary. But then you would burn your fingers.
At this point in his reasoning the results of an earlier experiment came to Brüel's aid. Back in the early 'forties the factory had sought to produce a ceramic vacuum bottle which could take the place of the ordinary type in metal and glass. The attempt was dropped at the time but now the experiments were taken up again and this time they were carried to success. The factory actually succeeded in welding together two porcelain cylinders, one inside the other, so that a heat insulating cavity was formed between them. On the following pages as we journey through the factory we shall see how it was done.

Production of the 'Thermodan' coffee pot begins in the model workshop. In the picture opposite Axel Brüel is seen working in the shop. In the foreground are the original models of the inner and outer bowls.

To the right of these the modelmaster, Egon Mortensen, is trimming the relief on the sides of the pot. The model is made of plaster. Note its large size; during drying and firing it will shrink about 20 per cent.

On the basis of the original model the modeller makes a working model like the one shown here. From this model a number of model forms are made over which the molds are cast – as seen on the following page – in which the porcelain pots themselves are cast.

With each of the many conversion processes leading from the original model to the molds – which are necessary to obtain the number of molds that will give the factory a reasonable capacity – something of the precision of the original model is lost. Therefore the original must be absolutely exact and very carefully made if the final mold is to have any precision at all. This means that the work in the model shop demands the greatest skill on the part of the modeller.

In the picture the mold is open showing its three parts: two sides and a lid.

The working model is varnished so that the mold, after casting, can be removed. Nevertheless, little by little the working model becomes worn and a new one must be made from the original model. If the original were used as a working model it would soon be damaged and the task of modelling a new one would have to be repeated.

In the plaster-casting workshop a large number of the molds that are used in the final casting with porcelain clay are made. Here, copper jugs are used in order to avoid rust spots in the plaster which might discolor the porcelain.

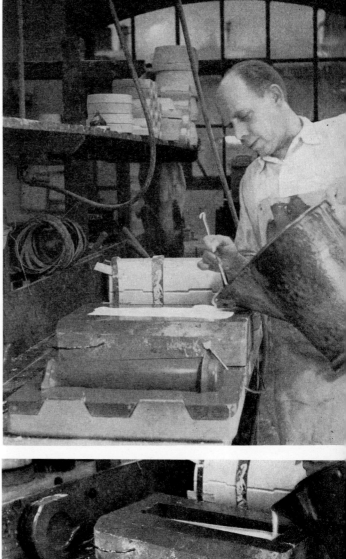

The coffee pot is cast in three parts: *1)* the outer bowl, *2)* the inner bowl with bottom, *3)* the bottom for the outer bowl.

The casting of the individual parts is very similar to the casting of the molds and consists in pouring a liquid mixture of porcelain clay and water into the absorbent mold. The water in the mixture soaks into the mold leaving a uniformly thin deposit of clay on the inside of it. The thickness of this layer depends on the length of time the mold absorbs the liquid from the mixture. In this case the filled mold stands for *10* minutes before the excess liquid mixture is poured off.

After several hours the clay deposit is dry enough to separate the mold and remove the pot.

In the picture at the left the three parts of a complete pot are being joined by 'gluing' them together with slip.

After the first or 'biscuit' firing at a temperature of 1650° F the pot is glazed.

To avoid the cracking of the pot during the final glaze-firing it must be glazed both inside and out as otherwise too great tension would arise in the brittle material. In a traditional coffee pot this presents no problem as both sides of the porcelain biscuit are easily accessible. But with the thermo pot it is also necessary to glaze the walls within the narrow cavity between the inner and outer shell. This is done with a spray which, with the help of a needle, is introduced into the cavity through a hole in the bottom of the pot (middle picture). The glazing of the outside is done in the traditional way by immersion. This process demands a great deal of experience and a steady hand. With a rapid – but steady – motion the pot is dipped into the glaze solution in a large tub. It is held only a moment under the surface and when it is taken up again its sides are covered with an even, soft coating of the glaze with no drops adhering and no rings showing (picture at right).

In the next picture the glazed pots stand on a drying shelf ready for the final firing.

68

The glaze firing takes place in a 280 ft. long kiln. During a little more than 24 hours the porcelain travels on a conveyer belt through the kiln. As the things move along they are slowly heated until they reach a zone in the middle of the kiln with a temperature of 2550° F. On the way out they cool off very slowly so that the change in temperature will not produce cracks in the material.

Opposite we see the coffee pot in use. At the center the diameter is just large enough for a grown-up's hand to grasp it firmly. The fluted decoration supports the grip and the raised rills makes the pot less warm there where it is held. Note that the contours of the pot are not straight lines, they curve out a little just as the sides of a classical column do. This is only a small detail but it gives vitality to the body; without it it would be a lifeless, geometric form. As the decoration is not carved into the surface but applied to the form like ribs, it strengthens the vital tension in the contours of the pot.

On the opposite page the entire coffee service is shown. As the one that is cut in half reveals, the cups also have double walls. The cream jug and sugar bowl have, of course, only single walls.

72

THE TEXTILE FACTORY

It has only been during the past few years that the Danish textile industry has attained artistic distinction. And, as in the case of the furniture industry, it has found some of its best designers among artist-craftsmen.

It is not always the young artists from whom new development stems. It is very often due to experienced craftsmen who have the results of many years' work in their particular branches on which to build further. A few young artist-craftsmen have done much for the Danish textile industry but its most significant renewal has come through Lis Ahlmann's fabrics in the Cotil collection of C. Olesen, Inc.

Lis Ahlmann's hand-woven textiles (see page 123) are closely allied to old Danish peasant weaving. Her striped and checkered fabrics are simple and unaffected patterns in white, brown and black, the natural tones of wool. When she uses other colors they are all subdued: unbleached white, deep brown, indigo, bottle green, navy blue. She has deliberately limited her color range so that she could concentrate the more on the textural possibilities of her colors and materials. Through this self-elected limitation the combined production of her hand-weavings forms a unique whole.

In the beginning of the 'fifties' Lis Ahlmann

73

joined the staff of C. Olesen, Inc., which is one
of Denmark's largest textile firms, and at the
same time she began collaborating with the furniture designer Børge Mogensen (see page 105).
Since then the two artists have carried out a very
comprehensive production of upholstery and curtain fabrics.

In the following we shall get a few glimpses of
the manufacture of two of Lis Ahlmann's and
Børge Mogensen's wool textiles designed for
upholstery.

The checkered fabric is made on a so-called
pick-à-pick shaft loom, a power-loom which is
constructed almost exactly like the traditional
hand-loom. A comparison of the picture on page
30 with the ones here will show that the individual elements are almost the same: the warp-beam, heddles, batten with reed, cloth-roller, etc.
The working of the two looms is also the same
only here the operations of hands and feet are done
mechanically. The picture below shows the way
the shuttle is cast into the shed with the help of
a shuttle-box which can work with up to seven
colors in arbitrary order. The shuttle is picked
up on the opposite side of the loom by a similar
shuttle-box which returns it after the shed has
shifted. On the opposite page is seen the back of
the loom with the large warp-beam. The warp
is kept taut with the help of a counter-weight
system which is connected with a brake drum on
the warp-beam. At the top are seen two small
spools which feed warp threads to the selvedges.

The textile factory's machinery and technical possibilities are not restricted to the comparatively simple pick-à-pick loom. There are many other types of looms for many different purposes. The picture here, for example, shows a loom operated by a Jacquard machine which can produce the most complicated patterns.

The Jacquard machine is mounted above the loom proper and takes the place of the apparatus we have already seen which produces the shed. From the machine here more than 3,000 threads are fed to the loom and each of these so-called 'harness' threads – just like the heddle 'eye-holes' on an ordinary loom – carries a warp thread. With the help of a band of perforated cards the machine alternately raises and lowers the individual warp threads for each pick, making it possible to build up even the most complicated patterns with large repeats.

The picture at left shows a section of C. Olesen's factory hall containing Jacquard looms. The perforated card machines are mounted on iron girders over the looms. We see the numerous threads which connect the machines with the warp threads on the looms and catch a glimpse of the band of cards hanging down alongside.

Lis Ahlmann's and Børge Mogensen's textile production is evenly artistic throughout, which is unusual in a comprehensive mass production of this kind. Every one of their designs is significant and taken as a whole their production represents a technical and artistic standard never before equalled in Denmark.

Supported by Børge Mogensen's masculine talent Lis Ahlmann has learned to utilize the huge mechanical apparatus and has succeeded in transferring many of the essential qualities of handicraft to the mass-produced wares without imitating handwork at any point. Her range of colors has become richer and her color schemes more daring but they still are never affected. Her designs have become bolder and larger. Thanks to her collaboration with Børge Mogensen, Lis Ahlmann's textiles have something in common with the best in Danish furniture design.

Lis Ahlmann's and Børge Mogensen's designs have hitherto been based exclusively on the simple weaving technique of the pick-à-pick loom but recently Lis Ahlmann composed a pattern for the Jacquard loom, a section of which is reproduced above in natural size. It clearly shows the way the weft threads are differently disposed for each pick.

On the opposite side is seen a section of the warp threads in one of the factory's large carpet looms which are still waiting to be seriously employed by designers of the caliber of Lis Ahlmann and Børge Mogensen.

78

THE TEXTILE PRINTING WORKS

Among Danish textile designers Rolf Middelboe is one of the experimentalists. In his first prints, made in his own workshop, the stress was laid on color. His patterns were rapidly and spontaneously carried out with free-hand brush strokes, with a spatula, or stippled on. But since he became connected with the textile industry several years ago, when he joined the staff of Unika-Væv, Inc., he has deliberately worked toward greater artistic precision, both in his patterns and his color schemes. His industrial prints do not rely on the charm which often results from the imperfect technique of hand-printing: the small variations in dyeing and the somewhat unprecise demarcations of the repeats which give life to hand-printed textiles. He has recognized that an article which is produced in hundreds of yards must be made with meticulous care, that its colors must be accurately determined beforehand if small accidents here and there are not to become more and more dominant as the production proceeds. The length that is printed today must be identical with the one which leaves the printing board a year later. All elements of chance have, therefore, been eliminated from Middelboe's work for the industry; everything is carefully determined and well planned beforehand.

The desire for greater precision and to gain absolute mastery over the production has made Middelboe particularly interested in patterns that are almost mathematically determined, patterns of similar, regular motives printed together in various ways. He has worked with circles, squares and — as in the fabric we shall watch being produced — with crosses.

The screen-printing stencil used here is, like Dorte Raaschou's (see page 34), made of silk gauze stretched on a wooden frame. The pattern can be transferred to the gauze in different ways: it can be drawn directly on the screen with lac or

chalk or the drawing can be photographed on to it. The latter technique is used here. The silk screen is covered with a thin coat of varnish which is again covered with a light-sensitive layer of bichromatic aluminium dissolved in gelatine. The design is drawn on acetate foil and then gone over with a lac that is impervious to light. The foil is then laid against the light-sensitive membrane and the screen placed under a strong arc light. This hardens the gelatine where the light penetrates the unlacquered parts of the negative. Under the lacquered lines the gelatine does not harden and can be easily removed with hot water. The design, however, is still covered with lac and not until this is removed (with lac remover) will the dye be able to penetrate the gauze. As only the hard layer of varnish is necessary, the gelatine layer is finally removed with ammonia.

And now the stencil is ready. The pattern appears as openings in the layer of varnish.

In the picture on page 80 Rolf Middelboe is working with the acetate foil. In the top picture on page 81 he is going over a finished stencil with lac and in the bottom picture on the same page the stencil for the first dye is lying on the printing table ready to use.

The printing table is about 150 ft. long with a solid top covered with three layers of felt and one of rubber sheeting which is waxed. Along the sides of the table run the two metal rails which partly carry, partly guide a trolley on which the stencil is mounted. Separated by the length of a repeat are stop blocks so that the stencil can be moved along the fabric in moves of exactly the same length.

In Dorte Raaschou's fabric (see page 34) the dye was applied with a simple rubber strip fitted in a wooden handle. In the textile printing factory here the 'doctor' consists of two strips of rubber with a thick roll of dye between them. These doctors are weighed down with lead weights and are equipped with long handles.

83

When printing, the printer guides the doctors, slowly and lightly, once forward and once back at each printing position. As in Dorte Raaschou's workshop Indigosol dyes are also used here.

In the top picture on page 82 the first color is being printed. Beneath it we get a close-up view of the stencil. In the one on page 83 the fourth and last color is being printed.

When all the colors have been printed the fabric length is hung up to dry under the ceiling. After drying, which is sped up by injecting hot air between the hanging lengths, the colors are fixed in a solution of sulphuric acid. Then the acid is neutralized in a soda solution and the fabric rinsed, washed, rinsed again, centrifuged and dried. The finishing ends by running the fabric through two steel rollers as hot as an iron which

roll against each other with a pressure of about ten tons. In the picture above the hanging of the printed fabric has begun.

Rolf Middelboe's curtain fabrics have been designed with special reference to present-day rooms with large windows and plain, precisely demarcated wall surfaces. In the print shown here – called 'Minisol' – he has succeeded in producing a design which, with its alternating translucent and opaque stripes, is able to neutralize the sharp transition from window opening to wall. Furthermore, he has made it possible to vary the design by, for example, placing two dark stripes or two light ones next to each other when sewing the curtains. Thus, even in so decorative a thing as curtain material, the design can be based on functional considerations.

THE CUTLERY FACTORY

New flat-tableware patterns are always appearing but very few of them have any influence on development; most of them are simply variations of well known types and as a rule the only change is in the decoration.

The many new sets appeal to the unfortunate passion for collecting 'patterns'.

The pattern called 'Obelisk', designed by the architect Erik Herløw, is different. Here, an analysis of use, material and production-technique has resulted in an entirely new form.

New thoughts regarding function, a new conception of the material and new ideas about production have always formed the basis of Erik

Herløw's work. This cutlery is not only characteristic of his own production but of the work of the new generation of designers who have taken up Herløw's ideals and working methods.

In 'Obelisk' the steel is not ashamed of itself, it does not try to imitate silver either in form, color or surface treatment. On the contrary, it exploits the advantages it has compared to silver: a hard, resistant surface and great strength which permits slender lines that, together with economic production, make it possible to sell the set at a competitive price.

From a technical point of view 'Obelisk' is entirely new in that each item is made in one piece.

86

In the first sets of stainless steel the knives alone were made in one but 'Obelisk' is the first in which all of the pieces are. And while hitherto stainless steel forks and spoons were made from plate steel all three pieces of 'Obelisk' are made from bar steel.

At the right is the raw material, bars of chromium steel imported from Norway. Steel can be tempered and its very high carbon content makes it robust.

The spoon and fork are made of the same hard material as the knife. Therefore the individual pieces do not differ from each other in form as is so often the case with stainless steel cutlery.

As in all mass production, the machinery for making 'Obelisk' is expensive and much preliminary work is necessary before production can begin. The making of the dies which transform the raw material – the shortened bars of steel, rectangular in cross-section – into useful instruments is exacting work. In the picture below are several of the dies used in making the tablespoon. In the foreground lie the dies which shape the handle and flatten out the bowl-end in a disk which later will be pressed into shape with the 'egg' shown in the background. On the opposite page the toolmaker is seen at work with his indispensable magnifying glass screwed tightly into his eye.

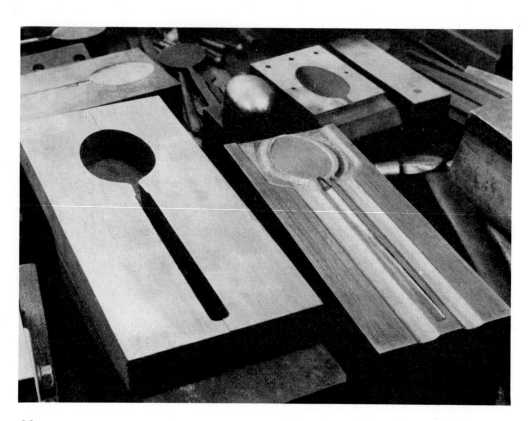

Heat, noise and dust; the Universal Steel Company's workshops are an inferno. In the open furnace the blanks lie ready, red-hot, in the fire. Sweat pours down the smith's glowing face. With a large pair of tongs he takes a blank and places it on the block. The heavy drop-hammer falls: once, twice, three times and once again the two dies meet. Every time they ram sparks fly from the red-hot steel. About 125 blanks drop from the machine during the 50 minutes the smith can stand the terrific heat. The high temperature forces him to take frequent pauses.

Under the stamping machine the roughshaped
spoons heap up; slowly they lose their glow and
become gray again.

The tremendous force with which the drop-hammer hits the steel creates tension in the material.
The molecules fly around in wild confusion and
the steel becomes as brittle as glass with a
tendency to splinter. By a subsequent heating in
a reverberatory furnace or over a gas flame, as in
the picture at top right, the tension is relieved
and the material regains its strength.

Already before the spoon bowl is shaped the
handle is given its first finish. The finishers sit
side by side at a long row of grindstones. The
driving belts from the electric motor under the
ceiling rattle as sparks fly and water drips from
the grindstones. All burrs are removed and the
handles given a mat sheen.

After being pressed into shape the bowl is given
a mirror finish and all edges are rounded and
polished. Each spoon is finished with such care
that it feels just as pleasant to the lips as a silver
spoon whose material is softer and more pliable.
Thus, as with other Danish industrial products,
it is the craftsmanlike finish which gives the
'Obelisk' set its high quality.

Above, we see in a glance the entire manufacturing process: first the steel bar and the blank made from it; next, the blank after it has been under the drop-hammer and in the stamping machine; again, after it has come from the reverberatory furnace. Finally, two stages of the finishing are shown: the bowl after shaping and the finished spoon in which the mat-polished handle forms a handsome contrast to the mirror-finish of the bowl.

On page 93 the complete set is seen. The balance in the pieces is excellent. The new manufacturing technique, based on solid handles instead of the usual hollow type, has made it possible to give the set the slim shafts which balance so perfectly with the lower part of each utensil. The pieces lay well in the hand and do not overbalance when placed on the edge of a plate. Furthermore, each piece is shaped so that the user is not forced to hold it in one particular way. The handles are rounded where the fingers rest

and flattened out toward the top to avoid rolling. The fork has only three prongs. Most older models have four but already in the 'thirties Kay Bojesen (see page 48) began – on the basis of a study of kitchen forks – to work with 3-pronged forks also for table use. He found that the 4-pronged fork with closely set prongs was disposed to split the food it pierced while the 3-pronged, more open, type could pick up food without breaking it. Since then many Danish designers have followed Kay Bojesen's lead in this and at the same time have designed the forks with a long, deep depression above the prongs so that sauce can be taken up together with the solid food. The 'Obelisk' knife is also based on Kay Bojesen's experiments (see page 122); its blade is short and its angle in relation to the handle makes it possible to cut with the entire edge. 'Obelisk' is industrial art of the same high quality as Arne Jacobsen's world famous dining-room chair which we shall meet further on.

THE FURNITURE FACTORY

Arne Jacobsen is undoubtedly Denmark's best known architect and probably the only one of international caliber.

He is not only a building architect but also one of our most productive industrial designers. During the past thirty years he has designed, among other things, furniture, textiles, wallpapers, glass, and eating utensils of stainless steel.

Most of the things he has designed stemmed directly from one or other of his architectural problems. They were designed to be used in a specific building and have only later gone into general production.

In architecture his constant striving for clear and simple architectonic expression has led him from the more impulsive to the severely restrained. As a result his buildings have become steadily more perfect but at the same time also more anonymous. This is also true of his industrial design.

The little dining-room chair which we shall follow through Fritz Hansen's Furniture Factory, is a text-book example of a cultivated industrial product. It is an extremely personal piece of furniture and its idea has been carried out with uncompromising consistency. It is at the same time elegant and one of the simplest pieces of modern Danish furniture ever produced. The

95

chair is popular because it harmonizes with other products symbolic of our time – scooters, 'baby' cars, enamel and stainless steel household articles. Like Fritz Hansen's stools on page 120 it is cheap and strong and, despite its distinctive form, comes close to the modern concept of 'the good, anonymous article of daily use'.

In the latest development in the field of Danish furniture most of the initiative has passed from the cabinet-maker to the furniture industry due to the decisive importance in the design of furniture of new materials and new production methods. Wood has not only lost its dominating position through the increasing employment of such ma-

terials as steel, glass and plastics but, as a result of industrial methods of treatment, wood itself has become a new material. Through veneering, bending and various pressure techniques wood has become plastic. The seat-back element of Jacobsen's chair is made of plywood, i.e. millimeter thin sheets of veneer, 'sliced' or 'peeled' off a log, which are superimposed one on another and glued together under pressure. The filling consists of eight layers of peeled veneer, which is the cheaper form, cut in a continuous slice from the periphery of a rotating log. The outer top and bottom layers are 'sliced' off as such diagonal sections give the handsomest veining. The picture

on page 95 shows the filling veneer bundled in large bales.

The first process in the production of the chair takes place on a belt-saw on which the rectangular sheets of veneer are roughly cut out (picture on preceding page). A suitable number of such pieces are placed together in the 'jaws' of a double templet which, like the jaws of a great monster, close together around the layers of veneer. The operator guides the templet towards the thin saw blade which is hung up over two large, rotating wheels and which descends vertically with great speed through a slit in the cutting table. With a humming sound the blade bites into the veneer and eats it away along the right side of the templet. The operator then turns the templet around with a precise twist and the saw cuts its way through the left side. The pieces that are cut off fly over the edge of the table into a scrap box; the shaped veneer is removed from the templet and stacked up by the gluing machine (picture above).

The sheets of veneer are now sorted, counted and placed in the right order.

In the gluing machine they glide between two rollers which coat them with glue on both sides; thereafter they are sent to the heart of the factory – the pressure press.

The chair factory's pressure press would be inconceivable in even the best equipped cabinet-maker's workshop. It is a very expensive piece of special equipment designed expressly for the chair type in question and can only pay its way in mass production. The pressure press operator is a specialist just as his colleague at the belt-saw is. Each one carries out the same simple process day after day and is therefore most effective from a production point of view, more effective than the furniture craftsman in the cabinet-maker's shop who employs his handicraft tools to solve constantly changing problems. The factory worker, through unceasing attendance at his machine, has become one with it.

At left the operator places the ten layers of veneer carefully in position between the two steel dies of the press. With a foot pedal he sets the suspended top part in motion and the dies slowly glide together as steam pours out of the opening between them.

After three minutes the dies again glide slowly apart and the flat pieces of veneer, now glued together, are transformed into a strong shell which is already hardened at full strength when removed from the press.

After gluing the degree of moisture in the plywood is quite high and therefore the shell must be allowed to dry out for several days before processing can begin (picture on opposite page).

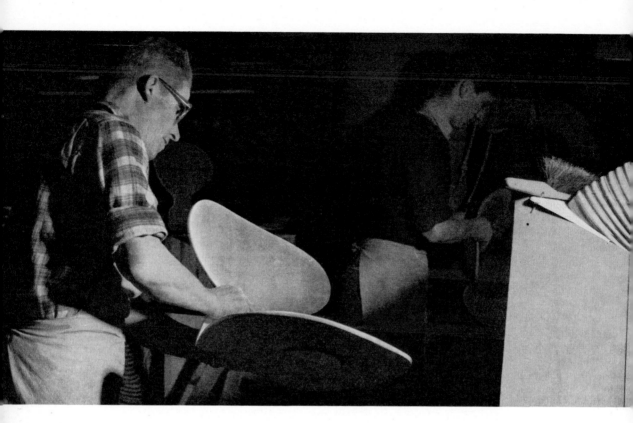

After drying, the shell is given its final shape in a milling machine. Guided by templets, the edges of the shell pass before the rotating cutting edge of the machine, first the seat, then the back. On the underside of the seat a round recess is cut out and a disk of plywood glued in. Into this are bored four metal bushes used in fastening on the leg element.

The disk is glued on the seat in an electrically heated clamping instrument.

The rough polishing of edges is done on a moving polishing belt, the final finish of both edges and surface with the help of a hand polishing machine, first with emery cloth and then with felt. The picture above shows the process at the polishing belt. In large, soft, undulating motions the shell is guided over the rotating belt until all edges are evenly rounded, without notches or splinters.

The flying sawdust is sucked up by the segmented tubes at the right.

A glimpse of the disk under the seat can be seen on the shell in the foreground.

The surface treatment of the shell takes place in a very warm spraying shop. The chair is placed on a rotating stand so the painter can get at it

from all sides without touching the wet surface. The shell is first given a ground coating and then sprayed three times with synthetic lacquer, each coating being ground down after hardening before the next is applied.

The fine mist from the painter's spray-gun can be faintly perceived. The minute drops are directed towards the shell; many fly past it or 'back-fire', filling the air and irritating nose and throat. But many drops are caught up again by the water in the floor basin and by the steady stream of it running down the rear wall of the spraying shop.

On the opposite page we follow the manufacture of the leg element in the factory's smithy. The legs are made of thin steel tubing. In the left-hand picture at the top of the page the tubing is lying on a storage shelf after being bent in an automatic bending machine. In the picture below we get a glimpse of the welder in his primitive canvas tent welding the tubes in exact position in relation to each other.

After welding the leg element is cleaned to remove any deposit left in the seams and then nickle-plated and its legs equipped with rubber tips and rubber stretchers; finally it is screwed to the disk beneath the chair seat (top right-hand picture).

Arne Jacobsen's chair – which the Swedes have named 'the ant' because of its characteristic silhouette narrowing in at the middle of the back – is a perfect example of a modern piece of furniture produced by modern technique for the needs of modern people. It fulfils its function of something to sit on and full advantage has been taken of the elasticity of steel and veneer. The chairs can be stacked together and they take up little space individually; they are cheap in price and strong in use; their shape is international but they are Danish in their fine finish and in the great care that has gone into their manufacture. 'The ant' is an industrial product but it has not been spewed out of an automat; its fabrication is followed by critical eyes from start to finish. Its resilient body has gone through many searching hands before it leaves the factory to be taken into service by the consumer.

104

SECTIONAL FURNITURE

In this visit to the firm which produces the 'B. B. Cabinet System' it is not so much the manufacturing process that is of interest but the principle of the design. The dimensioning of the B. B. cabinets is based on a long series of studies of the storage-space needs of ordinary households. These studies were inaugurated already in the early 'thirties by Professor Kaare Klint. Later, Børge Mogensen extended the investigations in his work with factory-made furniture and Grethe Meyer further developed these working methods in a number of studies made for 'Byggebogen' (a reference book for architects).

In the planning of the 'B. B. Cabinet System'

Grethe Meyer and Børge Mogensen have taken full advantage of the theoretical and practical experience gained from their investigations.

The 'B. B.' cabinets are a system of cupboards designed to meet every demand for storage space. Moreover, for each size of cabinet the two architects have worked out one or more standard interior arrangements to fulfill the needs most frequently met with. For instance, two cupboards, each about 3 feet broad, have been designed to hold all articles of clothing for respectively a man and a woman. On the opposite page the man's closet is reproduced and in the column to the right the contents of the four drawers are shown.

The construction of the B. B. cabinets is clear and simple and reflects the same thorough planning that characterizes their dimensioning. Though the construction is traditional every single detail had to be worked out in a new way to meet the special demands of sectional furniture. This is true, for example, of the fittings. In the series of pictures at top right are seen the hinges for the side doors which are made so that the doors have only to be opened 90° to draw out the drawers. In many of the older types of clothes closet the doors have to be opened almost 180° before the drawers can be pulled out.

The three lower pictures show the lock and key. The key, which also functions as a handle, sits in a recessed metal fitting so that it cannot scar a wall or neighboring cupboard it may come in contact with when the door is opened. Furthermore, one's sleeve cannot catch on the key in this type of lock. Hanging from the key to the storage space at the top is a leather handgrip.

106

The various elements of the cupboard are delivered unmounted; the sides and bottom are hooked together before the door frames are screwed on. On page 107 is seen a clothes closet partly erected. The sides, bottom and back as well as shelves and drawers are spray-painted with a gray enamel paint, the door frames are of Oregon pine and the doors themselves with teakwood veneer.

The over-all height of the cabinets corresponds to the Danish average room height of 8' 2" (2,5 meter), the interior height is the same as that of the average room door.

The B. B. cabinets were designed to meet the present-day demand for built-in cupboards to take the place of the free-standing ones that have hitherto dominated in Danish homes. The small size of modern apartments has made economy of space in the storing of clothes and household articles necessary while the rising standard of living

has not only created a demand for finer workmanship but has also brought about a greater interest in home furnishing and thereby a desire for furniture which harmonizes with the rooms.

To meet these demands, the B. B. Cabinet System has started production with cupboards designed for the storing of things every family possesses: clothes, linen and soiled clothing. The system will later be extended to include facilities for the storing of other things that are not necessarily found in all homes or that are found in varying quantities, such as books, magazines, writing, drawing and painting materials, musical instruments, sheet music, radios, record players, etc. A beginning has been made with the sectional shelves that are built with the cabinets seen above. Later on cupboards for all kinds of tableware will conclude the series. The B. B. Cabinet System is manufactured by Boligens Byggeskabe, Inc.

CHAPTER THREE: A CAVALCADE OF PICTURES

Our age has no special 'style' or, if it has, we are too close to the things in that style to be able to define it. Time has not yet, as in the case of the historical styles, separated the essential from the purely fashionable; we lack the long view. Today that which catches the eye is the individual form of expression. Style, which was once something general, has become something personal.

If we look for a common denominator in the work of Danish designers, it must be sought in the ethics of their work – in respect for material and respect for the problem to be solved.

In the previous chapters we have seen how the artists work with their materials, are inspired by them and give them form. We have seen that it is important, both to the artist-craftsmen and to the industrial designers, that they do not violate the natural potentialities of their materials and that in every case the materials stand for what they are: they do not imitate each other.

The same is true of production techniques. A casting must not look as though it were turned on a lathe; a machine-made product must not appear to have been made by hand.

But while the conscientious designer always looks on the fulfilment of the practical aims as his main problem, the artist-craftsman maintains his right to determine where the emphasis is to be placed in his work. In this he considers himself on an equal footing with the painter or sculptor.

A jug which is designed for mass production is a poor piece of work if it does not pour well, if it is hard to clean or if the handle is not easy to grasp. It is also a poor piece of work if it is so complicated to produce that it will cost too much. But the same does not necessarily apply to a jug that is made by an artist-craftsman in his own workshop, even if it is encumbered with the same functional defects. This jug must be judged according to the aim of the designer: did he intend to create a useful article or was his primary desire to give æsthetic pleasure?

Opposite page: A printed fabric designed by Dorte Raaschou for the Cotil collection of C. Olesen.

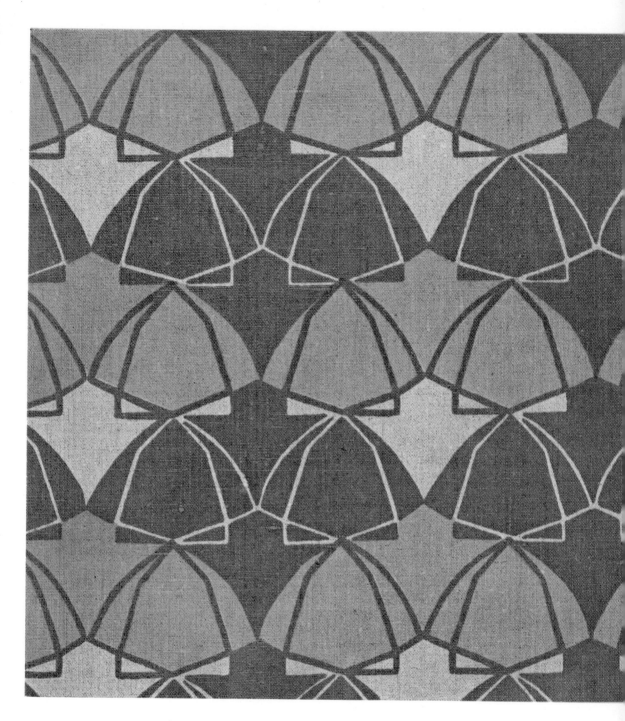

III

As a result of technical and social development, industry has become the dominating factor in the production of articles for everyday use. Nowadays there are few opportunities for craftsmen to work in this field. This development neither can nor should be stopped but it has, naturally enough, forced the artist-craftsman to seek his work in fields which were once the private domains of the artist proper. It has become more and more important for the craftsman to give us an artistic experience rather than to make things primarily for use.

In many countries this shift in emphasis has engrossed the artist-craftsmen to such extent that they have forgotten that they are not only artists but also *craftsmen*. A glance at modern Italian design will confirm this.

In Denmark we also have artist-craftsmen who seek inspiration from one or more of modern art's non-figurative forms of expression but they have not for a moment forgotten that they also are craftsmen. Even in their most spontaneous creations they have not neglected the elementary qualities of handicraft. Only after they have developed an almost faultless technique do they give imagination free rein. They never work the other way round.

The series of jugs on the opposite page are a good example af inexpensive, mass-produced utility wares. They were designed by Aage Helbig Hansen for the Danish Silver-Plating Factory 'Alfenide', Inc. The jugs, of stainless steel, come in two sizes $^1/_2$ and 1 liter.

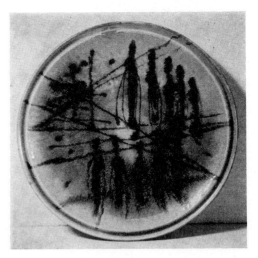

The platter to the right is an example of the unique, hand-made article in which functional efficiency is subordinate to æsthetic appeal. The platter, which was thrown on the potter's wheel by Grethe Lindblad, is covered with turquoise blue glaze on which the design is painted.

In the following chapter we have assembled a series of illustrations which show the scope of our subject – from the purely utilitarian object to that which aggressively forces itself upon us with an artistic message.

In our mind's eye we have seen the articles standing in a long row; farthest to the left are the anonymous wares, farthest to the right the purely decorative objects, each one unique of its kind. Or, in other words, to the left are the things that have solely a practical function, to the right those with a psychical function. In everything between the two extremes these functions will be combined: in some cases the functional is stressed, in others the æsthetic quality, but both are always present.

This arrangement, in which, naturally, it is impossible to place the individual elements precisely where they belong in the picture as a whole, tells nothing about the artistic values of the things in relation to each other. Because an article is placed far to the right – at the end of the row – it does not imply that the artistic contribution is necessarily greater than that of all the things preceding it. Moderation is not synonymous with mediocrity nor is restraint the same as dullness. Nor is the spontaneous piece of work by any means inferior to the sober and concentrated in which emotional force is barely suggested.

Magnus Stephensen's set of eating utensils at the left are sober articles of everyday use in the design of which full consideration has been given to their function and to a rational method of mass production. The fork and spoon are stamped out of plates of stainless steel and pressed into shape. The handles are slightly curved in cross-section which increases their strength. (A curved surface is not as easily bent as a flat one of the same dimensions). Stephensen's tableware is solid but does not feel heavy; the distribution of weight between handle and bowl is just right. The prongs of the fork are strong so that they will not bend when used and there is ample space between them so that the forks are easily cleaned. The bowl of the fork is deep enough to take up gravy from a flat plate. The blade of the knife is short and, due to its angle in relation to the handle, the entire edge can be used when cutting instead of only the point as is the case with traditional knives.

The set is produced by Georg Jensen Silversmiths, Inc.

On the opposite page are shown a series of water and milk jugs designed by Erik Herløw for Dansk Aluminium Industri, Inc. No jug could be simpler; its body is an ordinary cylinder shaped over a form (as on page 45) and furnished at the top with a broad pouring rim. The handle is the same as the one on the coffee pot on page 13. The jugs are shaped over a set of cylinder 'pistons' which are part of the factory's standard equipment; their heights were quite simply determined by the number of pistons that were necessary to produce jugs with cubic contents of respectively 1, $1^1/2$ and 2 liters.

The bottom picture shows a stainles steel coffee service designed by Magnus Stephensen for Georg Jensen Silversmiths, Inc. As seen here, the cylinder also lends itself naturally to hard steel. Here too the severe profile is only broken by the handle and spout, both of them small and pronounced.

116

The cylinder is also used in the ceramic industry. The lidded jars at the right were originally designed to be used in drugstores but have since also become popular for kitchen use. They come in sizes from 0.03 to 2.6 gallons. The jars are made of stoneware and have been produced since 1931 by the Hjorth family of potters on the island of Bornholm. Local material exclusively is used for both biscuit and glaze.

At the top of the opposite page are shown a series of plastic containers designed by Kristian Vedel for Torben Ørskov & Co. The containers, which are made of a hard, heat-resisting plastic (melamin), are equally useful in the kitchen and other rooms as serving dishes, jewelry boxes, ash trays, jugs, etc. They are available in black, dark gray, light gray and red.

Changed living and eating habits and changed technical conditions for the cooking and serving of food have resulted in the formulating of a new basis for the design of kitchenware and tableware. The manufacturers of pots and pans and the ceramic industry have been forced to design their products so that they would be suitable for cooking purposes and at the same time attractive enough to put on the table. The double-duty utensils at the left were designed by Jens H. Quistgaard for the United Iron Founders, Inc. They are made of cast iron and are all lined with a pearl gray glaze; on the outside they come in red, blue and black.

Opposite at the top is shown part of a wine service designed by Grethe Meyer and Ibi Trier Mørch for Kastrup Glasværk. The glasses shown here, for white wines, are produced in both transparent and dark green glass and are shaped so they can be stacked together, the flat-bottom bowl of one glass resting on the edge of the glass beneath instead of fitting into it. In this way the thin glass wall is not exposed to the outward pressure that arises in ordinary stacking.

Below at left are seen several pieces of a fireproof dinner service designed by Richard Kjærgaard for Bing & Grøndahl's Porcelain Factory, Inc. Being fire-proof means that, after firing, the material is able to expand so little that neither the porcelain nor the glaze will crack even if the dishes are placed directly over a gas flame or on an electric plate. Like Quistgaard's cast iron pots on page 116 these covered dishes are equally suitable for cooking and serving.
The shape of the service was determined by the desire to keep production costs down by avoiding 'split molds', i.e. molds which must be separated into several parts when the object is removed from it after casting. Here, the various pieces can be turned directly out of the molds. The service has a brown glaze on the outside and white inside.

Above is shown a fire-proof service with the same functions as Richard Kjærgaard's. It was designed by Magnus Stephensen for the Royal Copenhagen Porcelain Manufactory and the Faience Manufactory Aluminia. This service is also white on the inside while the exterior glazes are, respectively, yellow, brown and black.

Per Lütken's jug to the right is another sound, everyday ware, both cheap and serviceable. The shape of the handle makes it easy to hold in contrast to the usual ear-shaped handles that have been traditional for centuries. The jug is made of transparent glass by Holmegaard's Glasværk.

In the person of Herbert Krenchel the technician and the designer are united. Krenchel, who is a mechanical engineer, has not only made it possible to produce a form-pressed enamel bowl of millimeter-thin steel plate but he has also succeeded in giving his product perfect æsthetic shape. In the field of mass-produced wares these bowls are unsurpassed. They are manufactured by Torben Ørskov & Co.

Ingetoft's print on the opposite page is a textbook example of a good, cheap industrial fabric. As a yard-goods pattern it is ideal, consisting of a single, homogeneous color plane divided up by a rhythmically designed net of lines so that the design can be cut off at will without mutilating the pattern. Made by L. F. Foght.

The stacking stool at the left is also a perfect industrial product. It is simple and natural and so uncomplicated in form and construction that it can be said to have transferred the old handicraft conception of 'the good, anonymous article of daily use' to modern large-scale industry. It is made by Fritz Hansen's Successor, Inc.

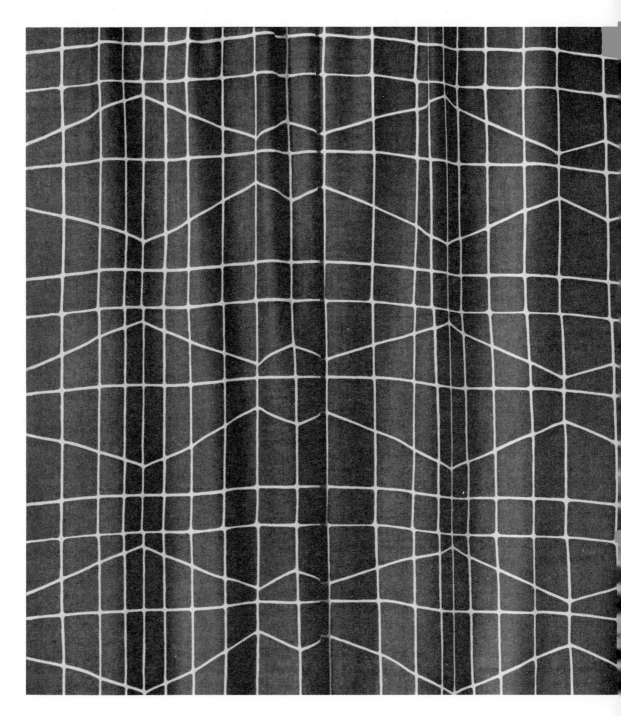

It was more than 20 years ago that Kay Bojesen first made this set of eating utensils. For Danish designers it has been a model of its kind because it has traits which will always be admired. All functional demands have been taken into account: distribution of weight, ease of cleaning, treatment of material, and design are all near perfect from a functional standpoint. Where the traditional form of the detail had its basis in function – e. g. the shape of the spoon bowl – that form was retained but in other details Bojesen rejected tradition. This is true, for instance, of the length of the handles which he made somewhat shorter than had hitherto been used. The same is true of the knife blade, the edge of which is also more curved so that more of it can be used for cutting. The set was originally produced in silver but later, with a few changes of detail, was adapted to stainless steel.

Also Lis Ahlmann builds on tradition, her point of departure being old Danish peasant weavings. The cotton tablecloth on the opposite page was first made in 1928. Its color scheme was inspired by colors found in a fishing hamlet: the ground is the reddish brown of the sail of a fishing boat, the four broad stripes are dark brown like tarred rope and the narrow ones the grayish white of fishing nets. The cloth measures 190 × 190 cm.

Beneath Kay Bojesen's eating utensils is a faience service designed by Magnus Stephensen for the Royal Copenhagen Porcelain Manufactory and the Faience Manufactory Aluminia. It is made especially to be used in places where it will receive harder treatment than faience is usually exposed to: the bachelor's home and the student hostel are its rightful surroundings. It is also designed to be used by children; therefore the edge of the plate is higher and slopes more than is usual and its glazes are very vivid.

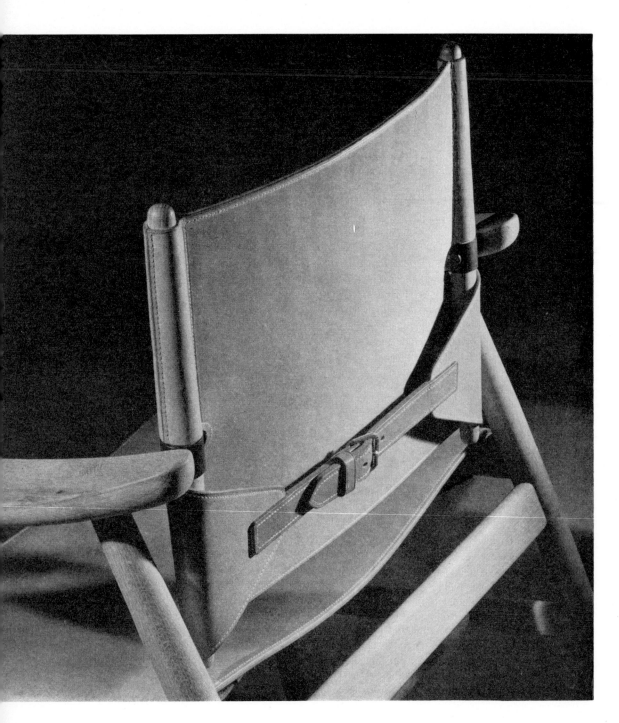

The upholsterer today seldom works independently. In the field of applied arts we usually find him in collaboration with furniture makers. In Denmark one aspect of his trade comprises all leatherwork and in this field things of the best quality are still produced independently, such as travelling bags, handbags, belts, harness, etc. (In Denmark the upholsterer is still called a saddle-maker).

Hitherto, aside from wooden furniture we have mainly seen everyday wares in industrial materials: stainless steel, aluminum, enamel and plastic, all of them materials which can form the basis of technically perfect products but they are limited by the fact that in textural effect they can reach no higher than to remain unchanged, unaffected by use. In contrast to these leather can stand as a good representative of the materials of handicraft which, when formed and treated in the right way, become handsomer with use. The textural effect of wood is enhanced, its color improved, under the influence of light and the wear and tear of years. The same is true of good leatherwork like the chair and sandals shown here. In each instance the product is an expert's solution of a practical problem but the textural character of the materials and the fine craftsmanship enrich the result.

In both instances the saddle-maker employed natural color oxhide.

The chair was designed by Børge Mogensen for the cabinet-maker Erhard Rasmussen, the leatherwork in both cases done by the saddle-maker E. & I. Dahlman's Successor.

In connection with the description of the B. B. Cabinet System on page 105 mention was made of Kaare Klint's exhaustive furniture studies. In the case of cupboards for the storing of tableware a beginning was made with simple experiments based on requirements. Klint and his students measured numerous models of the individual articles used for table setting: plates, cups, jugs, silverware; they found out how linen could be folded to take up least space, etc. From these studies Kaare Klint worked out a few basic sizes according to which the dimensions of shelves and drawers, and therefore of the cabinet itself, could be determined. Thus, the size of the sideboard on page 126 was based on 'standard tray-drawers', $14'' \times 21''$, which can hold two plates, 6 cake plates or 6 tea-cups and saucers, 12 coffee-cups and saucers, 24 glasses, etc. The sideboard, of Cuba mahogany, was made by the cabinet-maker Rud. Rasmussen.

The sideboard below was built on the same principles as Kaare Klint's sideboard. It was designed in 1958 by Børge Mogensen for P. Lauritzen & Sons Furniture Factory. The double-doors reduce the amount of clearage needed in front of the sideboard to a minimum.

Besides his large pieces of furniture which show English influence, Kaare Klint designed a number of chairs based on well known types from different periods and different lands but all of them completely renewed by Klint and all of the same simple construction. Thus, the chair at the top of the page was based on French and Italian peasant furniture. It is of beechwood, made by Fritz Hansen's Successor, Inc.

In the dining-room chair at the bottom of the page Børge Mogensen has further developed the type, creating a completely modern chair which, despite its robust character, is so light and takes up so little space that it entirely fulfils the modern demands conditioned by the small homes of today. The chair is made by FDB-Møbler.

127

The deck-chair is also an international type of chair. In the example shown here Kaare Klint has so carefully worked out all details that the mechanism actually works as it should. As seen in the lower picture the chair can be closed in a compact block in which the stringent curves fit perfectly together. The chair is an unpretentious thing to look at but nevertheless the finest craftsmanship has gone into its making. The frame is of teakwood with caned seat and back. The cushion is canvas covered, the carefully made metal fittings are of brass. The chair is made by the cabinet-maker Rud. Rasmussen.

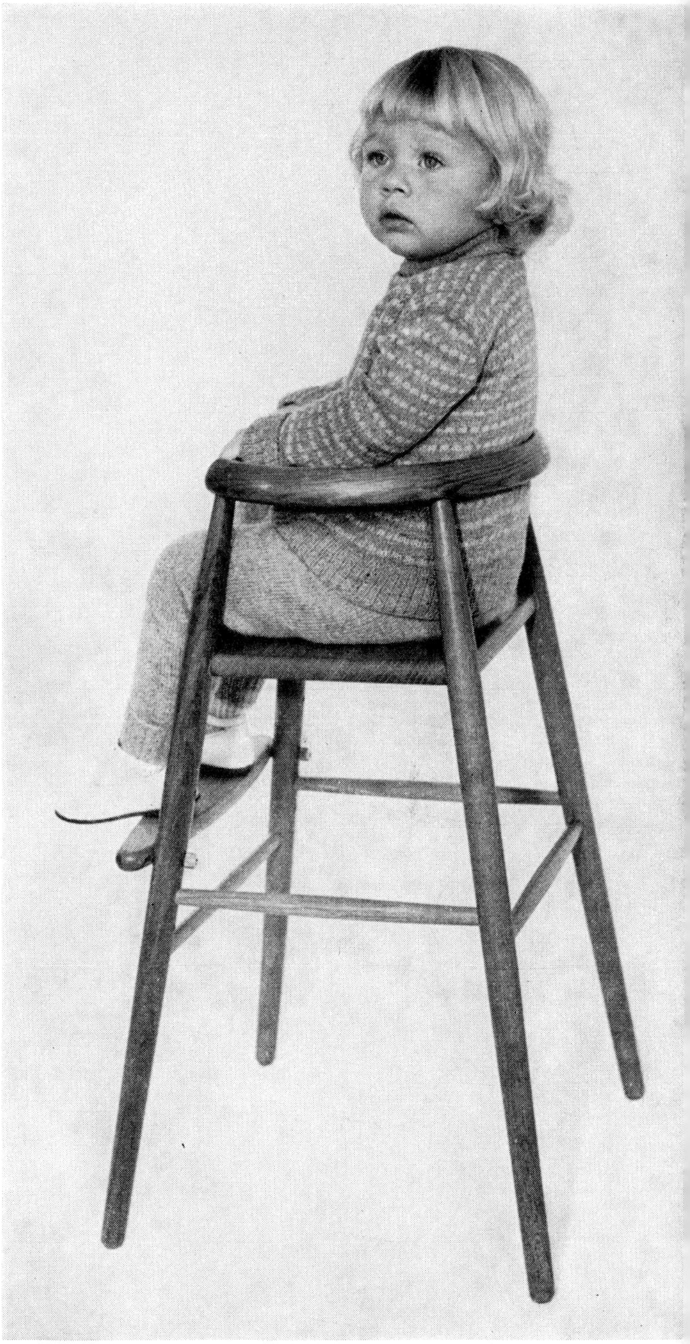

Kaare Klint laid the foundation for the Danish furniture designers' conception of furniture as unpretentious tools that should be pleasant to live with. In this nursery chair, designed by Nanna & Jørgen Ditzel, this conception is clearly expressed. The chair is made of oak by the furniture factory Kolds Savværk, Inc. The footboard can be adjusted at three heights.

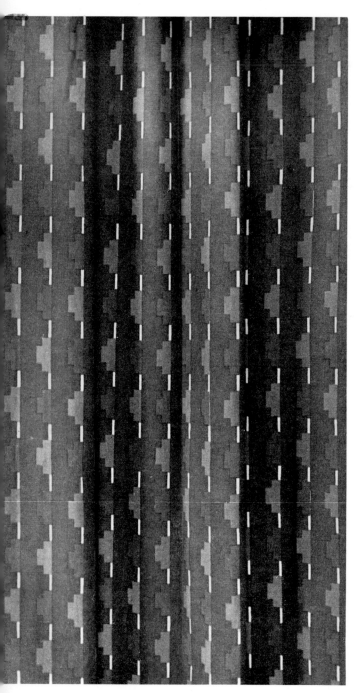

Poul Henningsen was one of the pioneers of
functionalism in Denmark and his lighting
fixtures clearly express the program of that
movement. The task of a lamp is to prevent the
eyes being dazzled by the filament in the electric
bulb and to throw the light from the bulb in the
direction needed. All of Poul Henningsen's
lighting fixtures are composed of a number of
shades which are shaped and placed so that they
conceal the bulb and at the same time throw the
light where it is wanted without the rays being
reflected more than once. On the opposite page is
one of Poul Henningsen's earlier lamp types.
Above is seen the newest edition which not only
illuminates the table under it but also gives light
to the entire room. These lighting fixtures are
produced by Louis Poulsen & Co.

Marie Gudme Leth introduced screen printing
in Denmark and her production has been of the
utmost importance for modern Danish textile
design. In her latest work she has concentrated
entirely on small-patterned fabrics which are
much used in interior decoration. With the help
of over-print technique she has extended the
coloristic possibilities of textile printing. In the
curtain material shown here she has exclusively
employed shades of brown.

Textile printing can be carried out in many ways. We have already seen examples of block and screen printing as well as combinations of the two techniques. But patterns – or elements of a pattern – can also be produced by dyeing.

In this wall hanging Ruth Hull first folded the material lengthwise in broad folds and then rolled it and tied the roll tightly about every 20 cm. She then dipped a number of the tied sections of the 'sausage' in a gray dye, untied the roll, folded the fabric in new folds, retied it and dipped it again. As the dye only faintly penetrates to the innermost folds, this process produces a ground pattern of rectangles in varying tones of gray. Over these Ruth Hull laid a new pattern of blue and brown rectangles produced by screen printing, and the composition was finally finished with black lines made with a brush. The width of the hanging is 3' 3".

The making of textile patterns by 'resist-dyeing' and 'tie-dyeing' are ancient techniques just as the making of earthenware pottery is an old folk art. Today earthenware is almost never used for household articles because the lightly fired clay is too fragile. But a small group of Danish ceramic artists have further developed the artistic exuberance which characterized the colorful work of the old potters. Among this group is Lisa Engquist who designed the jug shown on the opposite page. The jug was made by first throwing a vase and then pressing the clay together at the top in such a way that a smaller opening was produced beside the larger one. The 'web' between the two was cut away, separating the spout from the body. The jug is decorated with a yellow and white coating of slip under a transparent glaze. The slip was applied partly by immersion, partly with a brush. The jug is a perfect example of a shape which evolves from the technique employed in making it. It was not made from a sketch but grew naturally out of the clay under the potter's hands.

134

In this wall hanging – designed and woven by Vibcke Klint – the pattern derives from a special weaving technique: 'zig-zag' technique. Instead of casting the weft thread in a shuttle between the two layers of warp threads, as shown on page 30, the weaver rolls the weft thread up in a little ball and passes it through by hand. By this more laborious method the weaver is no longer forced to let the pattern colors go all the way across the panel but can break them off at will. Furthermore, if the warp is made of strong, fine yarn (e.g. linen thread) disposed at wide intervals and the weft of thick woolen yarn, the warp will be invisible in the finished fabric and thereby a 'pepper and salt' effect avoided. The colors in the zig-zag pattern are midnight blue, blue and unbleached white. The innermost triangles along the borders are red. The hanging is 3' 7" broad.

The stoneware bowl beneath the wall hanging is also decorated with a zig-zag pattern incised in the red stoneware. The glaze is green, the bowl 12" in diameter.

It was made by Gertrud Vasegaard for Bing & Grøndahls's Porcelain Factory, Inc.

Ancient Chinese pottery has of course influenced Danish ceramics just as it has ceramics the world over. This influence is clearly seen — both in the material and the shape — in the tea service shown here, designed by Gertrud Vasegaard for Bing & Grøndahl. The service is of porcelain covered with a lead glaze which was scraped off at the edges and replaced by a red iron glaze. The cup has no handle but curves down slightly at the top so that it cannot slip through the fingers. As the cup is large it is natural not to fill it and therefore it can be held without burning the hands. Both hands are used when drinking from it.

While earthernware is seldom able to fulfil modern demands as regards hygiene and durability, stoneware can easily hold its own beside faience and porcelain. When produced by modern methods it can compete in price as well. Nils Kähler has designed such a series of utility wares in unglazed and salt-glazed stoneware for the pottery firm of Herman A. Kähler. The unglazed teapots shown here are variants of a traditional shape evolved naturally from the technique of the potter's wheel. The material is a fine-grained clay which produces a surface that is full of life. The colors vary from a reddish brown to a very dark brown.

Chinese influence is also found in the Danish furniture industry. In this completely modern chair designed by Hans J. Wegner for Carl Hansen & Sons Furniture Factory the traces are faint but unmistakable, its lines going back, through earlier Wegner models, to Chinese chairs in the Museum of Applied Art in Copenhagen. The shape of the back-rest, the back-posts curved at the top and the broad, Y-shaped splat are all elements that originated in Chinese furniture design. The chair is made of oil-treated beechwood.

On these pages several more examples are given of Danish design showing Chinese influence, in many cases with English design as the intermediary. Their common traits are seen in the stringent form, the precise and delicate detail and the superlative textural treatment of each article.

Above is a silver teapot with a removable 'tea-egg', designed and made by the sculptor Henning Seidelin.

To the left is a salt and pepper set designed by Erik Herløw and made of ivory and ebony by I. G. Schwartz & Sons' Successor.

The chair on the opposite page was designed by Ole Wanscher and made of rosewood by P. Jeppesen's Furniture Factory.

140

The two furniture designers, Ejnar Larsen and A. Bender Madsen, have through the years consistently cultivated a few types of furniture, repeating the same structural and artistic motives again and again. In an exemplary fashion they have gradually perfected the individual elements, such as the sturdily framed cane-bottom seat of this elegant arm-chair. The frame is designed with due regard to strong construction where it is fixed to the legs and it narrows towards the center so that instead of being tautly stretched across it, the caning curves slightly towards the middle, making it comfortable to sit on. The chair, of rosewood, was made by the cabinetmaker Willy Beck.

Most Danish stoneware is produced by large pottery firms through collaboration between chemist, designer and thrower. Christian Poulsen is one of the few artist-craftsmen who produces stoneware entirely on his own. His work is simple and stringently modelled, of strong, robust material with thick glaze running down towards the bottom. In the example shown at the right he has employed a mat black feldspar glaze. The jar is about 16" high.

Besides working in silver, the sculptor Henning Koppel has also experimented with glass as shown in the large bowl at the right which he designed for Kastrup Glasværk, Inc. The bowl, which is 20" in diameter, is blown from the bottom and can actually be regarded as the lower part of a large broad bottle standing upside down. The domed bottom, curving up into the bottle itself, which is usually made so the bottle can stand securely — and to give a false impression of the amount it contains — has here become the inner shell of a large bowl.

In recent years many artist-craftsmen have given up light and fragile work to experiment with more robust forms. This is true of all branches of handicraft but the style change is most noticeable in pottery and furniture. At 'Saxbo' Eva Stæhr-Nielsen is one of the artists working in the new style, adding to the old production a new line of sturdy, robust wares of coarse-grained clay. The glaze is no longer smooth, half mat and soft as flower petals but thick-flowing and often glossy. The decoration is boldly incised or die-stamped. The glaze on the bowl shown here, which is about 16" high, is light green with under-glaze decoration in dark green.

Due to their frail construction Hans J. Wegner quickly abandoned rail-chairs for more solid and sculptural forms. On the opposite page is a folding-chair he designed in 1949, made by the cabinet-maker Johannes Hansen. The seat and back are of plaited cane. The chair is so simple in principle and so precise in form and construction that its mechanism seems entirely natural.

When an artistic contribution is added to the fulfilment of functional demands it is not the same as impulsive and spontaneous artistic expression.

For example, the three sober vases on the opposite page, designed by Jacob E. Bang, are certainly the result of artistic temperament but an artistic temperament that is guided by intellect. Their strict simplicity is not due to lack of imagination but to the artist's desire to express himself with honesty and restraint and without obtrusive artistry. The simple contours of the vases were by no means inevitable; they do not serve their purpose any better than a heavily decorated and opulently modelled ceramic vase would. Their form is deliberately æsthetic, the artistic cultivation of the spartan-like and chaste. The vases are produced by Kastrup Glasværk.

Similar ideals find expression in most fields of design. Below is an example from the furniture industry, a settee designed by Peter Hjorth and Arne Karlsen for Interna. It is composed of two arm-chairs set together, made of light oak with caned seat and back. The back-seat element can be adjusted in three different positions.

146

The frame of this rest-chair designed by Poul Kjærholm is made of a mat chromium-plated spring steel and, like ancient Greek chairs, its legs sway out at the ends so that the chair stands firmly on uneven surfaces. The seat and back are of wicker-work stretched between the two sides of the frame which are not joined together at the top of the back and edge of the seat as are chairs of ordinary construction. Instead, the wicker-work is strengthened at these places by a thicker edge of the material. Due to this non-traditional construction the seated person is not irritated by stiff rails behind the shoulders and under the knees. The wicker-work gives naturally under the pressure of the body.

Not every furniture designer can combine cold, hard steel with natural materials such as wood, leather or wicker. Poul Kjærholm can. The clear separation of the materials in the construction, the perfect textural treatment and the honest, craftsmanlike work make this combination of such different textures possible. The chair is made by E. Kold Christensen, Inc.

Arne Jacobsen is a versatile artist not only as an architect but also as an industrial designer. Besides furniture (see page 95) he has designed innumerable utility wares: rugs, upholstery and curtain materials, wall-papers, silverware, eating utensils, glass, porcelain, etc. As already mentioned, these things are often designed in connection with a specific Jacobsen building and later go into general production. At the right is seen one of his textile prints, 'Tasco', screen-printed by Graucob Textiles.

The glasses above have been given their characteristic profile not only on æsthetic grounds but also on functional ones. The bulge gives good support for the fingers when holding the glass and keeps the glasses firmly in position when they are stacked together. They are designed by Elisabeth Sass for Kastrup Glasværk, Inc.

This piece of nursery furniture, designed by Kristian Vedel, is both amusing and original, not simply grown-ups' furniture reduced in size but an original article based on the special needs and way of life of a child. In the slots in the laminated shell can be fitted a seat, a table top or an arm-rest for a standing toddler. Manufactured by Torben Ørskov & Co.

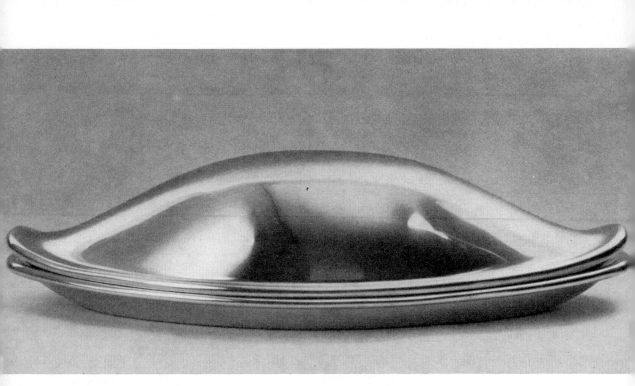

There is something attractive about a thing that is 'ageless', that has qualities of such universal appeal that generation after generation takes pleasure in using it.

Therefore, however, it does not follow that modernity is a negative quality. If the thing which is typical of its time is also good of its kind it will often be admired long after the generation that created it has passed away.

The objects on these two pages unblushingly flaunt the stamp of the Fifties. The covered silver fish platter above was produced in reaction against Functionalism's smooth, clarified forms but this does not mean that its design goes back beyond Functionalism to the period in which ornament was of greater interest to the designers than the things themselves.

In this platter Henning Koppel has further developed the material conception of the Thirties and Forties but instead of 'applying' decoration to the surface of the platter he has molded the object itself into a shape which has a decorative function altogether distinct from the utilitarian function of the platter.

The same is true of Hans J. Wegner's chair on the opposite page. The frame is a well known, simple and solid structure but the top-rail has been given sculptural character; it wholly and satisfactorily fulfills its function of giving good support to the back but in the vigorous molding and artistic utilization of the grain of the wood Wegner has treated his material as many modern sculptors do.

The fish platter is of sterling silver made by Georg Jensen Silversmiths, Inc.; the chair, of walnut, by the cabinet-maker Johannes Hansen. The platter is 28" long; the parted 'lips' at each end form the handles.

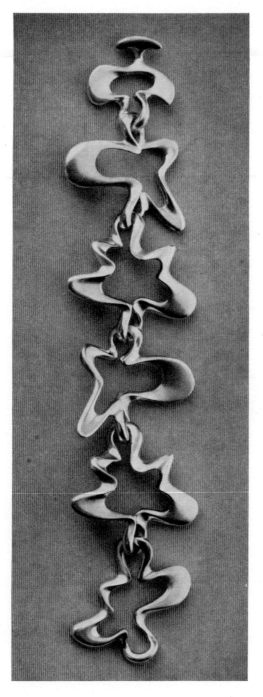

While many artist-craftsmen in their artistic expression approach the major arts more and more, a growing number of painters and sculptors – particularly the latter – are entering the field of utility arts.

Trained as a sculptor as he was, it was natural that Henning Koppel during his first years as a silver designer sought a place for himself in the design of jewelry where functional demands are comparatively few and not difficult to meet. Here, his abstract art, in which movement plays such a part, could most easily be further developed under the new conditions. But as a modern sculptor it was form and not surface ornamentation that interested him; it was the possibilities inherent in the material of creating a wealth of reflections and shadows that he wished to utilize. In this necklace made of sterling silver by Georg Jensen Silversmiths, Inc., each link is entwined in the following one, forming a single, flowing whole instead of being statically fastened together with the help of smaller links as in ordinary necklaces of this type.

Also furniture designers now and then move the emphasis in their design from function to artistic expression; many pieces of furniture are drawn sculpture worked out on paper in two dimensions. As an example of these somewhat exotic newcomers to fine Danish furniture design we show on the opposite page an ashwood chair designed by Vilhelm Wohlert and made by the cabinet-maker Arne Poulsen.

On the opposite page the ceramic artist Axel Salto is seen contemplating a piece of his work in one of the huge kilns at the Royl Copenhagen Porcelain Manufactory. From an artistic standpoint two persons have been chiefly responsible for the development in Danish ceramics: Axel Salto and Nathalie Krebs. Salto is the type of artist who works intensely to find his own artistic expression for the nature of things; Nathalie Krebs is the experimenter who, by scientific methods, strives to master the unpredictable material with absolute confidence (see page 17). Salto's work is always based on observations from Nature: sea-shells, snail-shells, pieces of flint, and particularly plant bulbs and seeds, have all inspired him. He has himself divided up his production in three groups which he calls the 'ribbed', the 'budding' and the 'germinating'.

The stoneware vase at the right, which is about 12″ high, belongs to the latest of Salto's three periods: the 'germinating'. His work in the two other styles, the 'ribbed' and the 'budding', express, just as this vase does, an inner strength but a strength dominated by the form. In this vase the smouldering life has broken out in long, thorn-like excrescences which have forced their way through the unity of the form. Guided by the varying lengths and shapes of the thorns the glaze flows like lava down the sides of the vase.

The bowl at the bottom of the page is characteristic of Salto's early work in the 'ribbed' style. The decoration is carried out as relief cut into the stoneware material itself and one with it. The glaze softens the relief and at the same time emphasizes it in that it adheres to the decoration in varying thicknesses, thinnest on the projecting edges and thickest in the shallows of the relief. Even after firing the bowl is reminiscent of the wet clay from which it was formed. It is not round; the sides, which were faintly pressed during the decorating, have taken their shape from the way the decoration is disposed around the bowl. The diameter is 10″.

155

Danish ceramic art has received many impulses from the modern schools of painting and sculpture that arose during and after the war. Thus, the potter Birte Weggerbye cultivates form in the same way an abstract sculptor does, expressing herself in the clay and glazes of her art in a way that appeals directly to the mind. She does not gather inspiration from Nature and is not influenced by natural forms. She creates freely and spontaneously, submitting only to her own ideas and moods. On her pottery weird forms conquer the surface, her decoration is like magic signs from primitive civilizations. The jar at the left, which is 23" high, is made of hard-baked red clay with white, black and gray-green decoration. The illustration above shows a detail from a decorated jug.

Textile patterns are also influenced by the ornamentation of primitive peoples. On the opposite page is seen a rug designed and woven by Anna Thommesen. The pattern is composed entirely of two gray and two faded green colors extracted from respectively pine needles and tansy. Anne Thommesen dyes her own yarn and employs only vegetable dyes.

Textile design is approaching the art of painting more and more. Today the materials used, alone, separate the textile designer from the artist proper. Thus, Tusta Wefring's work is closely related to abstract painting; the design on her wall hangings is actually applied to the fabric with a brush. Her compositions are carried out with dramatic strength in the lines and strong contrasts in her color schemes. In the wall hanging shown here an irregular net of black lines spreads over a ground composed of planes of light blue, three tones of yellow and three shades of orange. The textile printer Ruth Christensen might also be registered among painters. The designs on her wall hangings are not sketched or even planned beforehand. In every stroke of her brush lives the spontaneous suspense of the moment of creation. In the section of a wall hanging reproduced on the opposite page the ground is block printed while the line drawing over it was painted on.

158

Besides the color composition, the choice of yarns is an important basic element of the weaver's artistic contribution. In her pursuit of new textural qualities in yarns the weaver Paula Trock has worked up a minor business in which, with the help of small hand-worked machines, she makes raw wool into yarns suitable for hand-weaving. Her sensitive spinning brings out the special qualities and character of the various types of wool and produces a yarn which is lighter than the ordinary types.

In many of her newest fabrics Paula Trock has woven in a few glossy plastic threads in subtle contrast to the soft, fleecy wool yarns (bottom, right). And with this little, glittering extravagance we can fittingly pass from the field of handicrafts proper to one of the bordering fields: fashion.

The moment a fabric is cut up and sewn together to make a garment the basis for our evaluation of the fabric is essentially changed. The fact alone that the life-time of the things we are to judge — particularly when it is a question of women's wearing apparel — is very limited makes our fundamental views of quality appear too serious and, it cannot be denied, too dull. The demands we make on design in general influence our opinion of the fabric in a dress but not of its cut. Here, the artistic contribution does not have to have a deeper meaning for us to accept it. Integrity is not a sine qua non for the success of an evening gown.

Actual collaboration between Danish textile designers and Danish fashion creators is of very recent date. The first steps in that direction were taken when several young textile printers began on their own to make dresses of the materials they designed. Later, contact was established with the fashion industry and the dress shown here, created by the fashion designer Astrid Fog, is an example of this new collaboration. The material used, called 'wool spin', was designed by Paula Trock for the textile firm Unika-Væv.

The fashioning of fur garments is also one of the borderland industries. As is the case in most of the applied arts proper, responsible craftsmen and a guild stand behind the work of Danish furriers and hold in high respect the old traditions of the trade.

It can hardly be claimed that fur garments today have any practical function reasonably commensurate with their costliness. Those who can afford to wear fine furs are not forced to brave the cold and storms of winter and therefore the fur coat is no longer a protection against wind and weather. Today a fine fur coat is a lightweight garment, so soft and so handsomely made that wearing it gives the owner great æsthetic pleasure. It is an ornament like a precious jewel. As an example of Danish furrier work at its best we bring on the opposite page a persian lamb coat made by the furrier Birger Christensen.

We end our cavalcade of pictures of Danish handicraft and design with a few examples of modern Danish jewelry. In the design of jewelry æsthetic expression is all-dominating. Jewelry represents the superfluous, the unneccessary extra which makes life more colorful. Here, fantasy and light-heartedness are the only realities — beauty the only function. And yet the jewelry designer is not given a freer hand with his material than any other craftsman. Here, too, form must evolve from the special character of the material.

The necklace to the right at the top of the page was designed and made by Arje Greigst for Just Andersen, Inc. It consists of 52 cut stones of various colors which are mounted in such a way that they do not rest directly on the neck. As a result reflected light from the skin shines through the stones making the colors sparkle and glow. The bracelet at the bottom of the page, of gold, ivory and ebony, was designed by Erik Herløw for I. G. Schwartz & Son's Successor.

The qualities of a home as such do not depend on money. The essential thing is that the interior must grow naturally out of the way of life of the inhabitants and be in harmony with the tone that is used between them.

The picture on the opposite page can stand as an example of rooms which do not depend on purely formal qualities for their appeal but on human ones. We have deliberately placed it here as a contrast to the rooms on the following pages in which the 'home furnishing æsthetes' have made themselves very much more felt. Though it is the architects who have taught modern people to furnish their homes informally, the informal is often so strongly stylized at exhibitions and in architects' homes that the intentions seem throttled by the 'program' they imply. Too often such interiors resemble tableaux.

Behind the furnishing of the artists' home in which the picture on the opposite page was taken lies no æsthetic program, though the family's artistic work and interests have naturally left their stamp on the atmosphere of the home. Its charm consists of an informal arrangement of the possessions of two highly artistic people.

In contrast to the room opposite the interior to the left was very deliberately composed. Furniture, fabrics, lamp shades and even the pictures on the wall were chosen on the basis of a very clear and uncompromising conception of what a home should look like. Also in this case the things were acquired gradually; some are new, others old but every single piece was bought only after careful consideration. The rash purchases that many people make on the spur of the moment are not found in this home.

Almost all the furniture was designed by Kaare Klint. Some of the pieces were made by hand, others in a factory, but they go well together and with the other things in the room. For in furnishing a home it is not the origin or age of the things that is important but their æsthetic and structural qualities.

164

CHAPTER IV: DESIGN IN THE HOME

In the first chapter we maintained that no matter how beautifully a room has been designed by the architect, it is the things in it – the signs of human habitation – that are of first importance. In our daily surroundings we do not primarily seek a thrilling artistic experience but a feeling of security and comfort. It is said of the Danes that they are a friendly, unpretentious people and as the people are, so are the artists; only the exceptional among them succeed in breaking away from their generation and their milieu. This probably explains why the Danes have never formed the vanguard of a new artistic trend. Denmark lies on the edge of Europe far from the source of the great movements, not only geographically but also culturally.

Restraint, common-sense and sobriety characterize modern Danish interior decoration. It might also be described as *bourgeois*. But together with this outwardly negative unobtrusiveness, we find such positive characteristics as careful planning, high quality in materials and techniques, and naturalness in design. And that which is natural is never graceless or – even more important – never dull.

This picture of the Danish domestic interior does not of course apply universally.

Thousands of Danish homes are not very different from the average home in other countries with the same climatic conditions as ours and where, therefore, indoor life plays an important role. But the very fact that the home is of such central importance, has – supported by a rising standard of living – stimulated a lively interest in interior decoration. The original group which stood behind the demand for quality in domestic equipment has steadily expanded and has therefore been able to give our home-furnishing industries an economic basis on which to meet this demand. More and more Danes are not only 'cultural consumers' but also – though indirectly – cultural creators.

It is impossible to describe the ideal modern Danish interior; it simply does not exist. But in the illustrations in this chapter we have sought to show a number of characteristic themes which have been developed in an infinity of variations during the past decade. No single object illustrated is generic for its group but all of them include traits which, at one time or another, have influenced – or will come to influence – most people's ideas of what the modern home should contain.

No ordinary interior can show such consistency in its furnishings as most of those reproduced here. Almost all of them come from exhibitions or architects' homes and each interior was assembled, so to speak, all at once. No home which has grown naturally would be able to attain such perfection even though the inhabitants undoubtedly dream of it. Every home is a mixture of the changing ideals of different generations just as every home, fortunately, bears traces of the fact that several people live under the same roof. The atmosphere of a home is created by the interplay of these vital forces.

166

Cultural relics often play an important role in the home. It is both natural and admirable to hold in veneration fine furniture and other household articles that have been in the family for many generations. Often this feeling of deep respect for the living past – which has nothing to do with pretentious antiques or rare curiosities – manifests itself not only in old family possessions but also in the tone of the new furnishings.

In the middle of the last century a small group of Danish artists designed a number of pieces of fine, handmade furniture mainly to use in their own homes. Mostly, they were simple and well proportioned pieces, made of mahogany and in many cases decorated with inlaid motives in lighter colored wood in the neo-classicist style

of the period. Æsthetic impulses from that group have survived to the present day, thanks to – among others – Kaare Klint's early work (to which the chair at the right belongs). Even Mogens Koch's entirely modern sectional bookshelves against the rear wall in the picture reflects characteristic traits of that furniture from the nineteenth century. This is seen in their light dimensions, their smooth, precisely defined mahogany planes, their elegant details and fine craftsmanship in general.

Also the works of the present-day artists seen on the table and book-shelves in this room bear relation to the art of that 'golden age' of the nineteenth century. Therefore it can be said that this modern interior stands as a representative of a cultivated Danish tradition.

Despite unrest, war clouds and confusion caused by the onslaught of the technical world upon the boundaries of the feasible, our generation builds its homes on the same fundamental concepts our forefathers built upon. Family life is still the essential factor in the life of man. Let us therefore hope that the things *we* introduce into it may bear such a stamp of integrity and be so patently sound that the next generation will not cast them aside with contempt.

Let us hope that there always will be artists like those whose work we have seen in these pages and let us give them the sympathetic public which is a necessary condition for the flowering of the talent with which Nature has endowed them.

The Danish ideal interior is not showy and elegant but cultivates an atmosphere of sound bourgeois prosperity. When functionalism made its entrance in Danish home-furnishing it introduced plain, light furniture arranged in clearly separated groups, each with its definite function. But today furniture is again more solid and the purpose of the pieces more varied, and even in factory furniture stress is laid on textural quality. The close relation between indoor and out, which is the most positive contribution our generation has made to dwelling habits, has given furniture a much more robust character but has in no way lowered the demands for craftsmanlike qualities. The levelling of incomes by means of taxation has also brought about a change in dwelling habits. Homes have become smaller, housemaids have disappeared – and in many cases the separate dining-room with them – and this has resulted in increased interest in flexible, space-saving furniture. As to storing-furniture, built-in closets are more and more becoming part of the architecture of the room.

On the opposite page is shown a dining-kitchen designed by Børge Mogensen. The interior above was designed by Hans J. Wegner.

The room above is another example of a modern
interior in close connection with the outdoor
world but in this case the robust character is
modified. The invigorating informality of outdoor life is here united with the elegance of an
earlier type of dwelling; the summer house with
the old manse. In the many things on walls and
shelves, which reflect the interests of the inhabitants, and in the open fireplace we find again the
romantic strain in Danish interior decoration.
The chairs, designed by the owners of the house,
the architects Karen and Ebbe Clemmensen,

reveal the same double origin as the room itself.
In the slight frame with arms of leather straps
and the fixed seat-back element, the light garden-
safari chair is combined with the traditional
upholstered easy chair.

To be quickly accepted in a community one must
accept its conventions. New standards of conventions – including the artistic – are created by
those who are strong enough to ignore the existing
pattern. In the interior on the opposite page
Finn Juhl has not broken with the accepted

convention for the arrangement and use of furniture but, with complete disdain for all tradition, he has given his furniture an artistic stamp which denotes a definite break with traditional Danish design. These pieces of furniture derive their strength purely from the relation of their form to modern art.

In his most characteristic furniture Finn Juhl makes no attempt to adapt his design to the right-angled limitations of a room but strives to enhance the impression of the room with a sculptural accent. In his best chair types, therefore, he models the wood to the limit of its yielding capacity and gives his curves all the elasticity they can bear. These chairs do not lend themselves to mass production simply because furniture for the many, in order to glide naturally into any surroundings, demands – if not self-effacement – at least moderation and restraint. As an artist Finn Juhl goes his own way. He represents the spice in modern Danish furniture design.

All the furniture shown here was made by the cabinet-maker Niels Vodder.

The new Danish 1-family houses show influences from Japan and from Frank Lloyd Wright and also embody ideas from the German 'Bauhaus' school. But the cultivation of the textural qualities of the various materials, the scanty use of color and the honest craftsmanships, all go back to Kaare Klint's school and thereby to the Danish functional tradition. In all new architecture the desire to cultivate construction is evident — to leave it uncovered for all to see, to explore and utilize its æsthetic values. This same tendency also plays a significant role in furniture design and, in fact, in most branches of the applied arts. Perhaps this 'constructivism'–though it manifests itself in so many different ways – will one day prove to be the ideological conception which binds together all the products of modern design. Perhaps it will gradually crystallize into the 'style' of today.

The photograph to the left shows an interior from a circular house designed and furnished by Arne Jacobsen. The interior is characteristic of the 'cool' architecture of the Bauhaus group. The interior above shows the Japanese-American influence.

The furniture was designed by Poul Kjærholm.

PHOTOGRAPHERS

Th. Andresen .... 139 top
Bror Bernild 71
Christen Bloch 112
Durat, Paris 160
EB-Foto 63, 140, 143, 151, 169
FDB .... 127 below
Jørn Freddie 94, 158
Vagn Guldbrandsen 162
Gutenberghus .... 118 below, 135
Erik Hansen..... 13, 85, 104 right, 108, 120 top, 123, 126 top, 127 top, 128 below, 129, 134, 138 below, 141 below, 157, 171
K. Lund Hansen 15
Keld Helmer-Petersen 137, 146, 173
Ib Henriksen .... 118 top, 145, 148 top
Jesper Høm .... 104 left, 106 right, 107, 109, 126 below, 130 right, 153, 156, 168
Ingemann 116 top, 144, 148 below, 149, 161 top
Jonals Co. .... 6, 48, 49, 93, 115 top, 117, 121, 122 top, 124, 136 below, 138 top, 142, 155 below, 163 below
Erik Junior .... 39, 40, 41, 42, 43, 114, 115 below, 150, 152
Else Kjær .... 163 top
Mogens Koch 167
L. Meyerlist .... 161 below
Christer Nilsson .... 52 below, 53
Strüwing....... 4, 23, 51 left, 55, 116 below 119, 122 below, 131, 154, 155 top, 172
Svenskt Pressfoto .... 141 top
Else Tholstrup .... 103, 120 below
Anker Tiedemann.... 10 16 17 18, 19, 20, 21, 22, 24, 25, 26, 27, 28, 29, 30, 31, 32, 33, 34, 35, 36, 37, 38, 44, 45, 46, 47, 50, 51 right, 52 top, 54, 56, 57, 58, 60, 61, 62, 64, 65, 66, 67, 68, 69, 70, 72, 73 74 75, 76, 77, 79, 80, 81, 82, 83, 84, 86, 87, 88, 89, 90, 91, 92, 95, 96, 97, 98, 99, 100, 101, 102, 105, 106 left, 113, 125, 130 left, 132, 133, 136 top, 159, 164, 165, 170, 175

The sketch opposite the title page shows a jug designed by Henning Koppel for Georg Jensen Silversmiths Inc. The picture on page 4 shows a pot made by Lisbeth Munch-Petersen.

'Keglekrone' lighting fixture of copper designed by Poul Henningsen for Louis Poulsen & Co.

The authors wish to thank the many artist-craftsmen and manufacturers who have helped to make this book possible by the loan of photographs and critical reading of the finished manuscript.

'Made in Denmark' was translated by Eve M. Wendt. The lay-out of the book was composed by the authors. The text was set in Baskerville Monotype and printed by A/S Langkjærs Bogtrykkeri, Copenhagen, Denmark. The plates were made by Bernh. Middelboes Reproduktionsanstalt. The book was bound at the book-binding establishment of Anker Kyster's Successor, Bent Andrèe. The decoration on the cover is a reproduction of a textile print designed and made by Dorte Raaschou. © 1960 by Jul. Gjellerups Forlag.

Printed in Denmark